HIKING FROM INN TO INN

Wilderness Walking Tours
with Comfortable Overnight Lodging from Maine to Virginia

David and Kathleen MacInnes

Library of Congress Cataloging in Publication Data
MacInnes, David.
    Hiking from inn to inn.

    Includes index.
    1. Hiking—Northeastern States—Guide-books. 2. Hotels,
taverns, etc.—Northeastern States— Directories. 3. Northeastern
States—Description and travel—Guide-books. I. MacInnes,
Kathleen. II. Title.
GV199.42.N68M32   917.4   81-17336
ISBN 0-914788-49-3   AACR2

Typography by Raven Type

Printed in the United States of America

East Woods Press Books
Fast & McMillan Publishers, Inc.
820 East Boulevard
Charlotte, N.C. 28203

DEDICATION

To the multitude of men and women who have volunteered their time and effort to help clear, blaze and maintain the thousands of miles of foot trails in the eastern United States. They have, in the most important way, made this book possible.

Galehead

ACKNOWLEDGMENTS

We recognize the generous help of family, friends and acquaintances made on the trail. D H, D I and I F MacInnes helped us cover the five days of the Shenandoah Walk in one busy weekend. J T, M A and I F MacInnes hiked the Delaware Canal Walk with us on several blustery winter days, and the patriarch, J T, went on to reconnoiter the Catskills Walk with us and do one day of the Palisades Walk. G and D Foust helped hike the Sherburne Walk. B Mentzer gave us advice on the Cape Cod Walk, and we had the pleasure of her company for a day's hike. J Dolan and A Dryden hiked the Giant Ledges-Panther Mt section of the Catskills Walk for us, and M Harrison did the Cascade-Porter mts section of the High Peaks Walk. S Collins helped us update the Lakes-Madison section of the Presidential Range Walk while she and a friend were backpacking the New Hampshire and Maine lengths of the Appalachian Trail. R L Hagerman of the Green Mtn Club, G Lane of Bolton Valley and Z Norcross of Stowe gave us valuable first-hand information and suggestions for the Mansfield Walk. On the Sherburne Walk, both M and M Shonstrom of Churchill House Inn and R and F Schutz of the Tulip Tree Inn gave us valuable assistance. Bear, a stray black German shepherd dog, guided us over Mt Greylock.

H T O'Neill kept us from the worst of our literary gaffes.

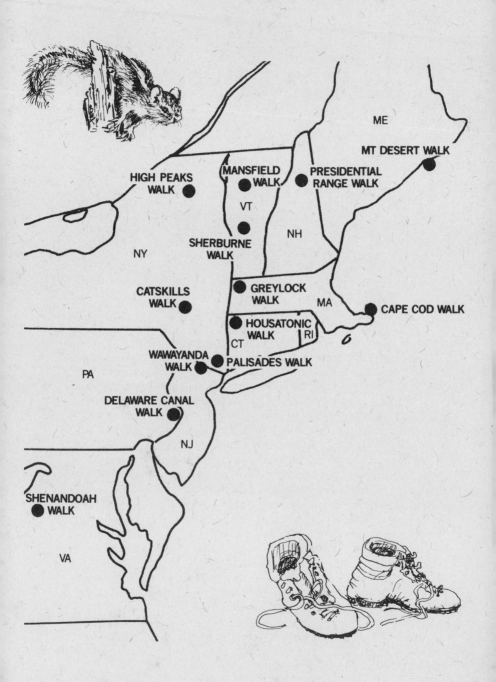

ME

MT DESERT WALK

HIGH PEAKS
WALK

MANSFIELD
WALK

PRESIDENTIAL
RANGE WALK

VT

SHERBURNE
WALK

NH

NY

CATSKILLS
WALK

GREYLOCK
WALK

MA

CAPE COD WALK

HOUSATONIC
WALK

RI

WAWAYANDA
WALK

CT

PALISADES WALK

PA

DELAWARE CANAL
WALK

NJ

SHENANDOAH
WALK

VA

HIKING FROM INN TO INN

CONTENTS

Acknowledgments			3
Introduction			6
Mount Desert Walk, ME	28.9 miles	3 days (circuit)	8
Presidential Range Walk, NH	47.6 miles	7 days	20
Mansfield Walk, VT	38.3 miles	4 days	40
Sherburne Walk, VT	43.8 miles	4 days	54
Greylock Walk, MA	26.9 miles	3 days (circuit)	64
Cape Cod Walk, MA	32.4 miles	4 days	74
Housatonic Walk, CT	41.9 miles	4 days	94
High Peaks Walk, NY	29.6 miles	4 days (circuit)	106
Catskills Walk, NY	26.7 miles	3 days (circuit)	120
Palisades Walk, NY	26.9 miles	3 days	130
Wawayanda Walk, NJ/NY	30.9 miles	3 days	142
Delaware Canal Walk, PA	45.9 miles	4 days	154
Shenandoah Walk, VA	39.1 miles	4 days	170

Notes
A	Public Transportation and Accommodations	181
B	Trailkeeping	184
C	Wilderness Manners	185
D	Wilderness Safety	185
E	What to Wear and What to Carry	186

Index	189

INTRODUCTION

We think that this book is a first of its kind in the U.S. Not only is it a working guide for the trails it covers, but it is also a guide to complete hiking vacations through some of the most beautiful countryside in the East. For too long we in America have thought that the linking of exciting off-road hiking with charming and comfortable lodgings was something only available in certain areas of Britain or Europe. This is not so. Out of the wealth of trails in eastern U.S., developed primarily for the day hiker or the backpacker, a substantial number can be linked to hospitable lodgings. Thus extended wilderness hiking tours are possible requiring only a light knapsack. This opens up to hikers and would-be hikers, who are reluctant or unable to backpack, the matchless pleasure of spending a series of days out of doors walking in splendid solitude while enjoying nights indoors in comfortable sociability.

The book is a guide to 13 of the more interesting of these hiking tours, ranging from Mount Desert Island in Maine to the Shenandoah Mountains in Virginia. They are each three to seven days in length, with a day's hike averaging 10 miles. Stealing from the British hiker categories of ambler, rambler, scrambler and dangler, we have selected trails for the rambler, with an occasional scramble where a hand or knee is needed. The hikes cover a great variety of scenic settings—wooded ridges, bare rock peaks and ledges, forested valleys, farmland, ocean beaches and rocky shorelines, canals and riversides. The overnight points have comfortable accommodations ranging from the old-fashioned country inn to the austere high huts of the White Mountains. Most are beautifully sited—in deep woods, on mountain ridges or in small towns. All the routes can be reached by bus, train or airline.

We stress that the book is a working guide, containing all the information needed to choose, plan for and undertake a hiking vacation. We locate and describe in general terms both the routes and the individual day's hikes so that you can visualize the nature of the Walks, their scenery and their degrees of difficulty. Each day's hike has the usual detailed trail description, but it is generally given for both directions of travel. We take especial care in describing difficult-to-find points on the trail, trailheads or junctions and note poor blazing. As a final service, we provide sufficient information about public transport and accommodations so that you can easily arrange your travel to and from the Walks and make reservations for the nights' lodgings. Each Walk (route) has a map showing the location of the trail relative to roads and towns, a help for reaching and leaving the trail and seeing how it trends. With the map of the route is a list of the sections (day's hikes), giving their mileages and overnight points. Where applicable the elevation climbed in each day's hike is given in the heading of the individual sections.

We have found a hiking tour to be an adventure in a way that other means of travel are not. Cutting yourself free from usual modes of transportation and relying for a prolonged period of time on your own two legs and your pathfinding ability return to you the inner reliance of your forebears. It is akin to their journeys. They set out, like you, to travel on foot by forest paths, over mountain trails and through open countryside. They stopped in much the same way you will, at small inns and other places, which provided human companionship, shelter, food and bed for weary travelers. The ease and speed of modern transport have blinded us to the advantages of such extended journeys on foot. The very fact that this mode of travel is arduous rather than effortless and that you give to it more than a day of your time means that you receive back in proportion a sense of achievement and a deep impression of the particular stretch of countryside over which you tread. This imprint can remain with you for life, a constant source of pleasure and satisfaction.

MOUNT DESERT WALK
Maine, 3 day circuit, 28.9 miles (46.6 km)

SECTION	DISTANCE		OVERNIGHT POINTS
1	8.7 mi	(14.0 km)	Bar Harbor-Otter Creek
2	8.6 mi	(13.9 km)	Otter Creek-Northeast Harbor
3	11.6 mi	(18.7 km)	Northeast Harbor-Bar Harbor

MAP—
AMC Map: Mt Desert Island (Acadia National Park). Order from Appalachian Mt Club, 5 Joy St, Boston, MA 02108.

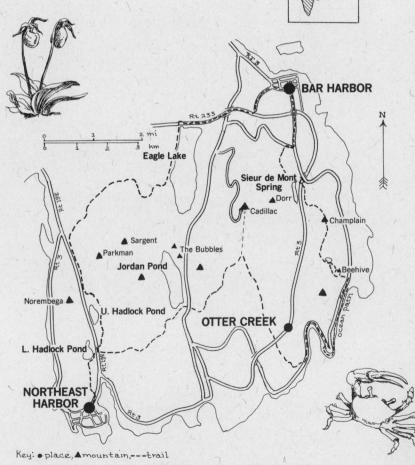

Key: ● place, ▲ mountain, --- trail

TRANSPORTATION
Bar Harbor—air (Bar Harbor Airlines), Boston; bus (Greyhound), Boston 1 r/t dly

ACCOMMODATIONS (area code 207)
Bar Harbor, ME 04609

Central House Inn, 60 Cottage St	288-4242
Cleftstone Manor, Rt 3	288-4951
Hearthside Inn, 7 High St	288-4533
Ledgelawn Inn, 66 Mt Desert St	288-4596
Manor House Inn, West St	288-3759
Thornhedge Inn, 47 Mt Desert St	288-5398
Town Guest House, 12 Atlantic Ave	288-5548

Northeast Harbor, ME 04662

Cranberry Inn	276-3702
Harbourside Inn	276-3272
Asticou Inn	276-3343
Kimball Terrace Inn	276-3383
Grey Rock Inn	276-9360

Otter Creek, ME 04665

Parkview Motel	288-5151

This hike is on Mount Desert Island, an island attached to Maine by a narrow causeway. Compressed into its 13 × 16 mile area are a mountain chain of 17 peaks from 200 feet to 1500 feet elevation; a rocky, heavily indented coastline; a fjord (Somes Sound); and miles of scenic car, bike and foot routes. The foot trails offer the best of all worlds—bare mountaintops easily attained, with magnificent views of other mountains and the sea; cool wooded valleys; mountain lakes; coastal paths and charming towns. The Walk is a circuit. It begins and ends at Bar Harbor, which is reached by bus and air from Boston and Portland. It goes south over a mountain and ocean footpath to Otter Creek, by another ridge over to Jordan Pond and thence through the woods to North-east Harbor, returning to Bar Harbor by a well-graded little-used carriage path.

9

There is so much to see and do on the island that we urge you to stay longer than the three days necessary for the Walk. Although there is no intra-island bus service other than a bus tour (which is useful as a quick orientation to the area), there is good taxi service, bike and moped rentals and lots of friendly people willing to pick up hitch-hikers. If you stay more than one night at Bar Harbor or Northeast Harbor, there are boat trips to be taken as well as fishing excursions. The Acadia Park Visitor Center, worth a visit, is difficult to reach on foot, but the Ocean Drive bus tour stops there.

OVERNIGHT POINTS

Bar Harbor, the largest and busiest of the towns on Mt Desert Island, is served by bus, air and water. In summer a mixed population of islanders, summer people and tourists crowd its stores and fill its streets. In spite of the crowd it is a place worth visiting, with period houses, a village green, and waterfront activities to enjoy. It is the home of the College of the Atlantic and the Jackson Laboratories, a center for the study of genetic defects.

You can take boat cruises (some accompanied by naturalists) among the islands of Frenchman's Bay in search of eagles, ospreys and seals, or go deep-sea fishing or sailing. You can take a full-day's ferry trip to Yarmouth, Nova Scotia and back, but there will be little time for sight-seeing at Yarmouth. You can walk through the West Street Historic District, past 17 turn-of-the-century mansions, or stroll along the Harbor Shore Path south from the town pier. The Historical Society, on Mt Desert Street, displays early photographs of the area. There are a cinema and many shops.

Northeast Harbor, once a fishing village on the eastern point of Somes Sound, was ''discovered'' in the 1880s by wealthy city people, and many of their large summer ''cottages'' survive. It has one of the finest natural harbors on the East Coast and is crowded with boats in the summer. You can take a cruise along the shores of Somes Sound and the Cranberry Islands to hear the history of Acadia and look for wildlife. The cruise lands on Little Cranberry Island to visit the Isleford Museum, with exhibits of the early history of ''Acadie.'' There is also a naturalist-led cruise to explore Baker Island. You can take a boat to Southwest Harbor, across

a native

Somes Sound, where there is the Oceanarium, a small "touch-me" marine museum. **Otter Creek** is a hamlet on Rt. 3 of some dozen houses, a store, post office and the Parkview Motel and Lighthouse Restaurant. **Sieur de Monts Spring**, while not an overnight point, has three attractions that you should not miss as you hike past: the Abbe Museum of Stone Age Antiquities, with prehistoric artifacts of the island; the Acadia Nature Center with its story of the island's flora; and the Wild Gardens of Acadia, displaying the native plants of the area.

NOTE ON ACCOMMODATIONS—In both Bar Harbor and Northeast Harbor there are many kinds of lodgings, but we have listed only those that might qualify as inns. Mt Desert offers much of this now-rare old-fashioned type of hospitality. Otter Creek has only one place to stay, so be sure to reserve well ahead of time. This advice also holds for the other towns if you go during the busy season of July and August. Be aware as well that some of the inns are not open year-round.

✓1. BAR HARBOR-OTTER CREEK
8.7 mi (14.0 km) / 1058 ft (322 m)

The outstanding feature of this hike is the variety of scenery it encompasses, certainly the greatest scope we have ever encountered in a single day's walk: a bare, wind-swept peak, deep forests, two lakes, a sandy beach and a stretch of rugged Maine coast. Starting at Bar Harbor you move from city streets to forest edge and go by woods and meadows to Sieur de Monts Spring, its ancient waters still bubbling clear. Here there are two museums and a wild garden to visit. Just beyond is The Tarn, a small lake that must have been named by a homesick emigrant from the English Lake District. Next is a climb up Mt Champlain to a bare rocky summit from which there are panoramic views of ocean, bays and other mountains. From the summit you go down to the looking-glass water of the Bowl and climb over the Beehive, a near-vertical descent by iron ladders and narrow ledges (this can be bypassed) to a sandy beach where you can sunbathe, swim and eat your pack lunch. You then have a leisurely two-mile stroll on the level Ocean Path, passing Thunder Hole, where the surf spouts with a roar, to the much-photographed Otter Cliffs. Leaving the ocean, you go through woods to the hamlet of Otter Creek.

The footing is good to excellent and the distance is not great, but you will feel you have had a full day since there is so much to see on the way.

11

Champlain Summit

SOUTH—From the village green in Bar Harbor, walk W on Mt Desert St and then S on Ledgelawn St 1.2 mi. At a fork go R to paved Ocean Dr (not signposted), and go R again to the first faint trail L (an old carriage path). Follow this 0.6 mi to Sieur de Monts Spring by keeping to the middle track at the first junction and soon passing a trail signposted to Dorr Mt. (If you miss the carriage path, continue on Ocean Dr 0.1 mi to signposted Jesup Trail L, and take this trail through very wet ground, flooded by beavers, to the carriage path.) Near the Spring the way is confusing, but you will see the buildings ahead. The carriage path leads to the N end of the parking lot for the museums; but you will recross the Jesup Trail (unmarked) just as the buildings come into sight, and go R.

Pass between the Nature Museum and the Abbe Museum and go S a short distance to the N end of The Tarn. Go L along the shore to Rt 3, 2.2 mi from Bar Harbor. Cross to stone steps of signposted Beachcroft Trail going E off Rt 3. At the top of the steps a dirt path ascends through woods and soon becomes paved with granite blocks. An easy trail for a Victorian lady, it goes by many switchbacks to a col between Huguenot Head and Champlain Mt, but it never quite reaches the summit of the Head. Halfway up the trail leaves the small woods and goes across a talus and bare rock to the col. From here the trail to the top of Champlain Mt climbs steeply at first over broken rock and then by living (bare, smooth, unbroken) rock to the summit (1058 ft) 3.0 mi from Bar Harbor.

The path from the col is much less distinct; watch first for rocks regularly relaid for your benefit and then for frequent cairns. From the summit you get a 360° view, E to the ocean, N to Frenchman's Bay, S to Sand Beach and Otter Cliffs and W to the rocky face of Dorr Mt and The Tarn below. From the top, the trail descends easily but by fits and starts, over mostly bare rock. The blue water of the appropriately named Bowl soon comes into view.

The path descends to and skirts this small lake. Notice the old beaver dam just above the natural dam of the outlet you cross.

A quarter of the way round the lake there is a fork; R leads to Gorham Mt and a route to Sand Beach that avoids the Beehive. The L fork leads over a knoll and down into a small ravine where you have your last chance to avoid the Beehive by going R. Keeping L you climb a short distance to the top of the Beehive, where you get close views of Sand Beach and the shoreline just below your feet! The trail now goes down the very steep SE face of Beehive. There are fixed iron rungs in critical places, and the only danger is from yourself. If you do not have a head for heights (by this we mean being comfortable when you look over your toes and see nothing but space for a long way down), do not take this route. Use either of the two bypasses. But if heights don't bother you, it is challenging to pick your way along ledges, down ladders to more ledges and finally to the broken rocks below. The reverse way is much easier as you don't have to look down. One guidebook calls it sporty. Norwegians would call it airy. It is, indeed, both.

Safely down by either route, go a short distance over level ground to the paved Ocean Dr and turn R. The sign to Sand Beach is immediately visible. If you want to swim, sunbathe or build sandcastles, go L through the parking lot to the beach. There is no good access from the beach to the Ocean Path which you take next, however, so it is best to return to the Ocean Dr and go E. You will soon reach the Ocean Path, a wide, level gravel path, generally below Ocean Dr and hence less noisy. Mostly in the open, the path offers views of the rocks and surf of the shoreline.

13

In about 0.7 mi you reach Thunder Hole, where the surf surges in a slot in the rock and, with proper surf and tidal conditions, spouts high in the air. (The first half of rising tide is said to be the best time for seeing this display.) It really does thunder, as we could hear it long before we reached it. Beyond the trail leaves Ocean Dr and goes through an open pine woods along Otter Cliffs to Otter Point, a place of quiet beauty (7.0 mi). The Ocean Path ends at the Point and, regretfully, you must go E on Ocean Dr. You pass the Fabre Memorial, a tablet to the memory of the commanding officer of a WWI Naval radio station, and go over a causeway where Otter Creek comes into the ocean. At 1.6 mi from Otter Point a wide gravel path goes R, unmarked, into Blackwood Campground. Take this path to the first paved road, and go L (it is the outer ring of one of the camping areas) to the signposted Cadillac Mt South Ridge Trail, which goes by a winding forest path 0.7 mi to Rt 3, just E of the entrance to the campground. Go R 0.4 mi to the village of Otter Creek and the Parkview Inn. The Lighthouse Restaurant is a few yds farther on.

Ocean Path

NORTH—Walk W on Rt 3 in Otter Creek to the signposted Cadillac Mt South Ridge Trail. Go L to a paved ring road in the Blackwood Campground and R to the first gravel road R. This leads you to the Ocean Dr. Go L over a causeway and along the coast to Otter Point (E point of the bay headed by the causeway), and take a path along the shore to the Ocean Dr just before Sand Beach. A short distance beyond the entrance to the beach take a path L (Beehive Trail). Go over or around the Beehive to the Bowl. Here you pick up the Champlain Mt Trail going N. Follow it to the summit and take the Beachcroft Trail down to Rt 3 and The Tarn.

Cross to The Tarn's N end to a trail leading N along the outlet to Sieur de Monts Spring (the Jesup Trail). Continue on this path;

pass between the Abbe Museum and Nature Museum to an old carriage path (about 200 yds beyond the museums), and go L. Some wet marsh trails intersect the carriage path but keep on, past the signposted Dorr Mt Trail. The Jesup Trail recrosses your way again in about 0.2 mi, but continue on the carriage path to the paved Ocean Dr. Go R to first road L, which will carry you in 1.2 mi into Bar Harbor. The village green and Main St are R.

2. OTTER CREEK—NORTHEAST HARBOR
8.6 mi (13.9 km) 990 ft (300 m)
This hike is another Mt Desert Island potpourri. It climbs through a mature forest of balsam fir and spruce to the open rocky spine of the southern ridge of Cadillac Mt, with magnificent views of the ocean and bays below, and descends a steep, rough wooded gorge to join an easy woodland path along the shores of Jordan Pond. Here the encircling mountains are mirrored in crystal clear waters. The last leg goes by a woodland path to the coastline and Northeast Harbor filled with sailboats. This combination of deep woods, open mountain ridges, lakeside, marsh and seacoast is matched by an equally diverse combination of footing. You will encounter soft pine-needle paths a pleasure to trod, other paths crossed by a myriad of roots waiting to trip you, exposed rocky ridges needing careful attention to cairns and boggy places determined to wet your boots. The most demanding part is a short but very steep scramble on a tumble of rocks where it is hard to believe that you are still on a trail. Except for this last section the way is easy hiking.

Jordan Pond is a good centerpiece. A well-known old restaurant there, the Jordan Pond House, was being rebuilt from a fire in June 1981 when we passed. Old patrons hope they will replace the

Jordan Pond

unusual birchbark walls of the original dining room. From this location there is a superlative view across the lake to the twin mounds of the Bubbles. Time your hike so you can enjoy your lunch here, either out of your knapsacks on the pond's edge or served to you in the restaurant. The last part of the hike down to Northeast Harbor follows along the base of a high dike of stone, resplendently clad in a huge cloak of mosses and ferns, a cool green paradise.

WEST—Leave the Parkview Inn in Otter Creek and walk 0.5 mi SW on Rt 3 past the Blackwood Campground entrance. Past the entrance 100 yds you will see stone steps going up both sides of the road; take the R (NW) one marked Cadillac South Ridge Trail into a forest of mostly balsam fir and red spruce. The trail ascends gradually to a signposted fork at 1.0 mi: the Cadillac Trail goes L, and the Eagles Crag Loop, which gives a splendid SE view over Northeast Harbor, goes R for 0.2 mi before returning to the main trail. From where the two trails rejoin, the way is over an open ridge with continuous beautiful views; the full panorama unfortunately is behind you. Keep a sharp eye for the cairns here since the trail wanders from one side of the broad ridge to the other.

You soon descend into the sag called The Featherbed and reach the Cannon Brook Trail crossing (2.7 mi, signposted). A pond, filled with the song of bullfrogs when we passed, is L of this junction. Go L on the Cannon Brook Trail and in a short distance you will be plunging down a steep ravine. It is very rough underfoot and the track is scarcely different from its surroundings, so take care—watch your footing and for the small cairns. As you come down the last steep cleft in the great rock face you will see a red metal marker on a tree L. The trail levels out and bears L around a torn-up open area made by beavers long ago creating a pond and a food supply. Look for another red marker on a tree, easier to see coming the other way. These red markers, shaped like birds, will now appear at infrequent intervals to guide you to a distinct path. You will be paralleling a carriage path on your R which you will glimpse occasionally and finally cross. The Cannon Brook Trail ends at the Pond Trail at 3.3 mi, and the latter carries you to Jordan Pond (4.6 mi). The Pond Trail is a joy to walk on after your struggle down the Cannon Brook Trail. When you reach Jordan Pond, there is a self-guided nature loop L (pamphlets in a box here) that is worth the small digression. Otherwise go R and walk along the path that soon bends S following the shore of the pond past Jordan Pond House to the carriage path just W of the dam.

Go L on the carriage path to where two wooden bridges cross Jordan Brook. (If you stop at Jordan Pond House, there is a short trail which leaves from the NW corner and meets the carriage path at this same point.) Cross the first and smaller of the two bridges and find just beyond two trails. Take the L fork marked to Asticou. It is a carefully made trail, wide and smooth for some distance. You will cross several carriage paths, pass an active beaver pond and climb a long set of granite steps. There are a number of forks in the trail, each carefully signposted; keep to the forks marked to Asticou until, at 1.8 mi from Jordan Pond House, a faint path goes R, signposted to Hadlock Pond and the Gatehouse. Take this path for 0.5 mi, past another fork (signposted), through woods and along the edges of a cemetery to Rt 198. There are small cairns along the way since the trail is faint. Cross Rt 198 to a path. When the path crosses a powerline, go R down to the shore of Lower Hadlock Pond and L to a dirt road along its S shore. Go W on this road, and when it forks go L away from the lake. At the next fork go R. In a short distance three trails will be signposted together on the L. Take the middle trail, clearly marked to the village (the Skiddoo Trail). The trail ends in 0.8 mi at Rt 3. Grey Rock Inn is 0.1 mi R and the Harbourside Inn 0.1 mi beyond. The boat harbor and Kimball Terrace Inn are another 0.3 mi farther on, down the first road L. The Cranberry Inn is 0.5 mi L from the trailhead, on Rt 3 beyond its junction with Rt 198.

EAST—Walk E on Rt 3 about 0.5 mi from Northeast Harbor to a set of steps going L uphill and which reaches a dirt road in 0.8 mi. Go R to Lower Hadlock Pond to find a path along its E shore. Go R under a powerline to a footpath L leading to Rt 198 (1.7 mi). Cross to a path on the other side of the road, and follow signs to Jordan Pond (4.0 mi). Take the Pond Trail E to Cannon Brook Trail (5.3 mi), and climb to the intersection with Cadillac Mt South Ridge Trail at Featherbed (5.9 mi). Rt 3 is R (8.1 mi); Otter Creek is 0.5 mi L.

monarch butterfly

3. NORTHEAST HARBOR—BAR HARBOR
11.6 mi (18.7 km) / 400 ft (120 m)

Northeast Harbor

The network of carriage paths built by J. D. Rockefeller early in this century, when he heard that cars were going to be allowed on the island, goes through some of its loveliest parts. They are so much a part of Mt Desert that we have chosen to lead you back to Bar Harbor by some of them. You can imagine the carriages rolling along these paths on a summer day and may even wish yourself in one. Not open to autos, the paths are still used for horseback riding, of which you will be reminded by hoofprints and other signs of horses if not by the horses themselves.

You retrace your steps from Northeast Harbor and take a carriage path around the base of Parkman and Sargent mts past a small marshy pond to Eagle Lake, thence along the lakeshore to an auto road leading to Bar Harbor. The way is mostly through the woods and thus is shady and cool on a hot summer day. The footing is firm gravel on the carriage paths, and each intersection of the multitude of paths is well signposted. Except for the stretch along Eagle Lake which is surfaced for bicyclists, the paths are rarely used, and you will probably have the day fairly to yourself.

NORTH—Walk NE on Rt 3 from Northeast Harbor to a set of steps marked to Hadlock Pond, going L into the woods and ending in 0.8 mi at the S end of Lower Hadlock Pond. Go R around the lakeshore, first on a dirt road and then by a path to a powerline running E. Go up the line until it crosses a path, and take the path L to Rt 198 (1.5 mi). (If in doubt, continue under the powerline a short distance to Rt 198, and jog L.) Go L on Rt 198 a short distance past a substantial gatehouse, and go R through the smallest of a set of massive gates to the first carriage path. Go L; the path skirts Upper Hadlock Pond and continues N for several miles parallel to but at some distance from Rt 198. It finally swings NE and at 5.0 mi passes a trail to Parkman Mt. In another mile it swings E and passes along the N side of an un-named lake and climbs gradually to a junction at 6.5 mi, marked L to Betty Pond and straight ahead to Eagle Lake. Go straight and then L to Eagle Lake on a finely graveled path; you may encounter some cyclists. The path goes down a mile to the shore of Eagle Lake and turns L along the shore.

In 1.5 mi you pass under Rt 233. Turn R immediately after the underpass to reach Rt 233 (Eagle Lake Rd, 8.9 mi) and go E. It joins Rt 3 at the outskirts to Bar Harbor. Take Rt 3 into the town center.

SOUTH—Go W out of town on Rt 3 to Rt 233 (Eagle Lake Rd), and go on the latter to the NW end of Eagle Lake (2.7 mi). There is a parking lot on the R (N) side of the road with a path leading W to the carriage path. Go L (S) on the carriage path which will veer away from the lake in about 1.5 mi. At 5.1 mi leave the finely graveled section, and go R on a less well-tended carriage path. Follow the signs to Hadlock Pond until you reach Rt 198 through a set of gates (10.1 mi). Jog L to a path going R into the woods, and follow the WEST trail description of Section 2 from this point to Northeast Harbor.

mountain ash

PRESIDENTIAL RANGE WALK
New Hampshire, 7 days, 47.6 miles (76.7 km)

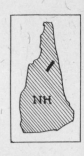

SECTION	DISTANCE		OVERNIGHT POINTS
1	2.5 mi	(4.0 km)	Franconia Notch-Greenleaf
2	7.5 mi	(12.1 km)	Greenleaf-Galehead
3	7.0 mi	(11.3 km)	Galehead-Zealand Falls
4	5.5 mi	(8.9 km)	Zealand Falls-Mizpah Spring
5	4.7 mi	(7.6 km)	Mizpah Spring-Lakes of the Cloud
6	7.3 mi	(11.8 km)	Lakes of the Cloud-Madison
6a	4.5 mi	(7.3 km)	Lakes of the Cloud-Pinkham Notch
7	6.1 mi	(9.8 km)	Madison-Pinkham Notch

MAP—

AMC Maps: No 3 Franconia (Sects 1, 2, 3 & 4), No 2
Presidential Range (Sects 4, 5, 6, 6a & 7). Order from Appalachian Mt Club, 5 Joy St, Boston, MA 02108.

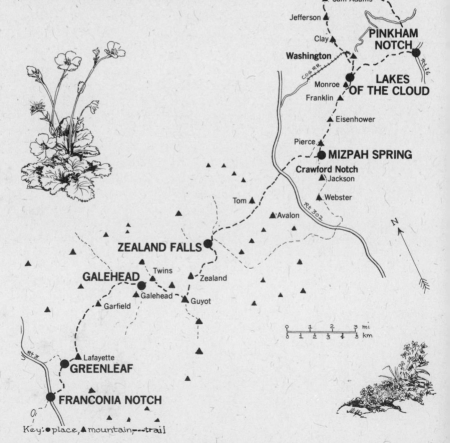

Key: ● place, ▲ mountain, - - - trail

20

TRANSPORTATION
Franconia Notch—bus (Concord Trailways), Plymouth, Concord
& Boston 1 r/t dly
Pinkham Notch—bus (Concord Trailways), North Conway, Con-
cord & Boston 1 r/t dly

The Appalachian Mt Club operates a hikers' shuttle in the summer between **Pinkham Notch, Crawford Notch and Franconia
Notch**, 1 rt/dly except Thurs, leaving Pinkham Notch early am
and returning in pm; write AMC, Pinkham Notch (address
below).

ACCOMMODATIONS
Appalachian Mt Club huts (for description see p 22). For reser-
vations call or write Reservations Secretary, AMC Pinkham
Notch Camp, Gorham, NH 03581, tel. 603-466-2727.

This is one of the premier hikes in the eastern United States, with
miles of walking above treeline and endless views. It is also
strenuous hiking and should be attempted only by those who are
fit and have had some hiking experience. The trail leaves Franconia Notch and swings through the Pemigawasett Wilderness to
Crawford Notch, thence by the great ridge of the Presidential
Range to Pinkham Notch. You will cover 15 peaks over 4000 feet,
six of them the highest summits in the Northeast. You will stay in
six of the seven high huts of the Appalachian Mountain Club, a
unique experience described below. If the weather is clear you will
have all sorts of viewpoints—ledges, cliff edges, bare mountaintops, the long tundra-clad ridge of the Presidentials. There will be
dim, leaf-green tunnels filled with ferns and mossy rocks down
which delicious ice water drips. You will pass crystal cascades with
pools just foot or body sized to cool you. You will encounter the
marvelous smell and delicious comfort of sun-heated pine
needles. At night you will make new friends and rejoin old friends
from the previous hut.

Lakes Hut

THE HIGH HUTS—The AMC Hut System, the only one of its kind in the U.S., is a series of remote, rustic, catered lodgings, high in the White Mountains, which enables you to travel long distances through deep wilderness without carrying heavy packs or camping out. Only serious hikers reach the huts and there is thus a commonality of interest and a camaraderie seldom found elsewhere. The huts are austere, but hearty family-style meals, bunks with blankets and pillows and the cheerful kindnesses of the young men and women who run the huts make you forget the lack of amenities. The hut experience is unforgettable—living with people who share tired muscles and enthusiasm for the mountains, hilarious skits put on by the hut "croos," informal evening naturalist programs, friendships that carry from hut to hut and even into the outside world, delicious meals made more so by the day's strenuous exercise, and ready hands and hearts to help those in difficulty.

Since so much of the route is above treeline, the weather is sometimes severe (even in summer there can be high winds, low temperatures, rain, sleet or snow). You should always carry clothing appropriate for late fall travel elsewhere. In addition, you will need a sleeping sack or sheet and a flashlight (no lights in the sleeping rooms and no lights elsewhere after 9:30 pm). You will have to carry food for your lunches as the huts do not provide them. But you can buy candy bars and sometimes fruit there.

If you are uncertain about being on your own on these somewhat formidable trails, the AMC offers a series of overnight hikes using the huts, led by experienced guides. The groups are kept small and include all ages and backgrounds.

All the huts are open from mid-June through August, and some through October.

22

TRAIL MARKINGS—You will be much less dependent on paint blazes for this Walk than for any other. First, the trails are well used and carefully maintained, so they are highly visible underfoot. Second, when walking below treeline, the surrounding forests are so dense you could rarely stray off the trail even if you wanted to, and the trails are very well cairned above treeline. Third, all trail junctions are well posted, so you will always know which fork to take. Because of these factors you will find the blazes often very far apart. In season the trails are well used, and you will pass more friendly fellow hikers than on most other trails.

OVERNIGHT POINTS

Greenleaf Hut (4200 ft), often called Sunset Hut, is on a treeline knoll overlooking small Eagle Lake; it faces the tundra of the long Franconia Ridge, and offers superb views of Franconia Notch and the mountains to the west. Eagle Lake is a good example of a lake well on the way to becoming a bog. The hut was built in 1932 and is one of the smaller ones, with a capacity of 36. **Galehead** (3800 ft) is on a little wooded hump at the end of the long Garfield ridge, with a good view over the Pemigawasett Wilderness, the last area logged in New Hampshire because of its difficulty of access. The scars of the old logging roads are still visible along the sides of the ridges. It is the most remote of all the huts, and strenuous hikes are required to reach it. It was also built in 1932 and has a capacity of 38. **Zealand Falls Hut** (2700 ft) is in Zealand Notch beside the lovely cascades of the Whitehall Brook. The smooth brookside rocks are perfect for sunning and the pools just right for soaking tired feet or, for the hardy, the rest of the body. (Do your soaking below the hut, please, since your drinking water comes from above.) The sound of the brook will lull you to sleep at night. The water will soon provide a good portion of the hut's energy requirements through a small hydro-electric plant being installed as we passed in 1981. The electricity generated will replace much of the bottled gas which is presently lifted in by helicopter. Zealand Notch got its name from early lumbermen who called the general area New Zealand because of its remoteness. Hut capacity is 36. **Mizpah Spring Hut** (3800 ft) is the newest and most elegant of the high huts; its sleeping quarters consist of eight rooms with 4 to 10 bunks in each, rather than the more standard two large bunkrooms. The hut is in a clearing in the woods on the E flank of Mt Clinton, and it has views of the Dry River Wilderness and the Chocorua Region. Capacity is 60. **Lakes of the Clouds Hut** (5050 ft) is the highest, largest and busiest of the high huts. Well above treeline in the col between Mt Washington and Mt Monroe, it has spectacular views west into Ammonoosuc Ravine and, on a clear day, across to the mountains of Vermont and Canada. It is often in the clouds with visibility reduced to yards, and the temperature is often in the 50s with winds of 50 mph. The high winds and short growing season reduce the few trees to bonzai proportions. Patches of snow linger into June and snowfall may surprise you in August. The hut takes its name from two small lakes nearby (the nearer one is your water supply so please keep your feet out of its ice water, and swim, if you are foolhardy, in the farther one). The hut was first built in 1915 but has since been enlarged. Its capacity is 90. **Madison Hut** (4825 ft) is on the site of the first high hut, built by the AMC in 1888, and is in the Madison-Adams Col. Its lichen-covered stone walls and grey-weathered shingles blend into the landscape. The hut is not easy to reach, and you feel a strong sense of isolation there. Good views are obtained by a 10-minute walk east or west. The small Star Lake, so named because it reflects the stars at night, is a short distance away. The hut was rebuilt in 1940 after a fire. Its capacity is 50. **Pinkham Notch Camp** (2000 ft), located on Rt 16, is the headquarters for the hut system, and you will either begin or end the Walk here. It was originally built in 1920 and has since been greatly enlarged. Though in the style of the high huts, it has smaller numbers of bunks in the rooms of the sleeping quarters, sheets on the beds and hot water (ah, luxury!). A pack-up room downstairs in the main building is open 24 hours a day for hikers not using the camp to stop in, relax, shower and repack their gear.

Crawford Path

ALTERNATE ROUTES—Not everyone will have the good fortune to be able to take seven consecutive days to do the whole walk. Under our rule that public transportation must be available, the route can be divided into two four-day hikes by using the new Appalachian Mountain Club shuttle from Pinkham Notch (see Transportation, p 25) and hiking either Franconia Notch to Crawford Notch or Crawford Notch to Pinkham Notch. A three-day circuit from Pinkham Notch is also possible using Lakes of the Cloud and Madison huts; you reach the Lakes Hut from Pinkham Notch through Tuckerman Ravine (see Section 6a). Other combinations are possible as there is a multiplicity (we might say a bewilderment) of trails feeding into the main route we follow, but we have not worked out for you the transport problems involved.

If you are taking the full seven-day route, we recommend that you take an extra day along the way to rest and absorb more of the surroundings. Zealand Falls Hut is our first choice for such a stop. It is a midway point, its location beside the falls and in the woods is pleasant for resting and a number of short hikes from it offer mild activity.

1. FRANCONIA NOTCH—GREENLEAF
2.5 mi (4.0 km) / 2440 ft (744 m)
This is the shortest stretch of the seven-day hike, but the distance is deceptive since you climb steeply most of the way. You can arrive at the trailhead as late as mid-afternoon, if your travel plans so dictate, and still make supper at the Greenleaf Hut. This is served at 6 pm sharp as it is at all the huts, and nothing will be left for the tardy because appetites are unabashedly gluttonous. If you are new at hiking up substantial elevations, you might allow two and a half hours to cover that distance and altitude comfortably.

This hike is a fine introduction to the Presidential Walk. You travel up from the deep Notch to above treeline on an old bridle trail which once served the hotel that used to crown the Lafayette summit. The trail goes up the back of a steep narrow spur of Lafayette, first through a deciduous forest, then through spruce and balsam that grow steadily more stunted as you climb, until it arrives at the almost treeless knoll on which the Greenleaf Hut is perched.

EAST—Directly opposite the entrance to Lafayette Campground on Rt 3 in Franconia Notch is a small kiosk, a billboard and numerous trail signs. The Bridle Trail goes L from the kiosk. In summer a ranger may be stationed here to answer questions and issue warnings if the weather is severe. The trail to Greenleaf is protected by trees or shrubs from high winds and is therefore quite safe. The trail starts in the White Mtn National Forest, a birch-maple forest, and goes by an easy grade first SE and then N. In about 0.8 mi it levels off briefly and then begins climbing fairly steeply up the SE spur of Lafayette. The trail now becomes rocky. You get partial views R into Walker Ravine and across to Franconia Ridge, which stretches S from Mt Lafayette, and at a sharp L turn you get a fine view of Mt Lincoln. The deciduous forest soon begins to be replaced by stunted spruce trees. Shortly after the view of Lincoln the trail runs along the W side of the spur on open ledges, and you get fine views of Cannon Mt with its aerial tramway and of Lonesome Lake across the Notch. Beyond you begin the last steep climb to the hut.

As the roof of the hut comes in view, so does Lafayette and the whole sweep of the Franconia Ridge. The hut is perched above a small mountain lake with the mile-long slope up to Lafayette's summit beyond.

WEST—Leave from behind the Greenleaf Hut on the Bridle Trail S, which leads you down a long spur of Lafayette to Franconia Notch and Rt 3.

Greenleaf

2. GREENLEAF—GALEHEAD
(7.5 mi (12.1 km)/2240 ft (680 km)
We can report that these are long and very strenuous miles. This is not to daunt you, for it is a fascinating trail, but to warn you not to be taken in by the seemingly short distance. We were forewarned but were still surprised at the time it took. You leave Greenleaf and climb to the summit of Lafayette. You will be in the open for more than a mile. You then hike all the long wooded

Garfield ridge, which involves climbing Mt Garfield and most of Galehead Mt. There will be frequent views of the Garfield ridge ahead or behind and occasional outlooks of the surrounding mountains. The trail over Lafayette is a marvel of engineering and remains so in places but relapses into mud, roots and rocks at the eastern end. There is the faint remains of the TipTop House on the summit of Lafayette to puzzle over. It was built in the mid-1800s to satisfy the penchant of the Victorians to reach difficult places; it was struck by lightning and burnt down in 1911. Now there is left only the foundation and the stone corral of the ponies that once carried up the well-dressed patrons. We passed it in heavy mist and were unable to see anything of the ruins.

Galehead

EAST—From the S corner of the Greenleaf Hut take a blue-blazed trail E which drops down to the level of small Eagle Lake and then climbs through spruce and balsam before coming out on tundra. Continue to climb fairly steeply to the summit of Mt Lafayette (5249 ft) where you meet the Franconia Ridge and Garfield Ridge trails, 1.1 mi from Greenleaf. Go L (NE) on the Garfield Ridge Trail, blazed white, which you will follow all the way to the Galehead Hut. The trail dips slightly and then climbs to the lesser N peak of Lafayette (1.5 mi) from where it makes a long, gradual descent. At 1.8 mi you pass Skookumchuck Trail on your L (3.6 mi down to Rt 3) and soon after cross the treeline. From this point you remain entirely in the woods except for the summit of Mt Garfield, but there will be frequent narrow views ahead and behind.

At 2.8 mi you reach a col and climb over a hump to a second col at 3.7 mi, the latter a tangle of downed trees. Now you begin to climb gradually toward Garfield. At 4.1 mi you will pass Garfield Pond and from there climb the steep, rocky, wooded cone of Garfield (4488 ft). The trail passes just N of the summit at 4.6 mi. Galehead Hut is visible from here when the weather is clear; it looks close but is actually 3 mi away. From the summit you descend equally steeply to a trail junction in 0.1 mi. The Garfield Trail goes straight ahead here (5.6 mi to Rt 3), and your Garfield Ridge Trail goes R. Beyond this junction a side trail leaves L for the Garfield Ridge Camp site. You continue ahead, cross a small brook and reach a col. Just beyond, at 5.4 mi, the Franconia Brook Trail leaves R. From here to the hut the Garfield Ridge Trail does a devil's apprentice dance for 2.0 mi, up and down in short spurts, with never a honest yard of easy walking. At 7.0 mi the Gale River Trail comes in from the L (5.8 mi to Rt 3). Finally at 7.5 mi you arrive at the junction of the Twinway Trail, with the Galehead Hut a few yards to the R.

WEST—The mileage points are Gale River Trail 0.4 mi; Franconia Brook Trail 2.0 mi; Garfield Trail 2.7 mi; Mt Garfield 2.8 mi; Garfield Pond 3.3 mi; Skookumchuck Trail 5.6 mi; N summit of Lafayette 5.9 mi; the main summit 6.3 mi. Go R from the summit on a blue-blazed trail to Greenleaf Hut.

from Zealand

3. GALEHEAD—ZEALAND FALLS
7.0 mi (11.3 km)/1100 ft (335 m) E, 2200 ft (670 m) W

This section follows the Twinway Trail over South Twin and Guyot mountains and the Zealand Ridge to the deep V of Zealand Notch. There are frequent views of the Pemigawasett Wilderness and peak on far peak along the skyline dominated by Mt Washington. Both the mountains over which you pass have bare summits, and the views are superb. In addition, there is a cliffside eyrie on the edge of Zealand Notch which looks out over a deal of empty air to Mt Washington and the intervening ridges. It is a relatively easy walk compared to the Greenleaf-Galehead section,

It has much better footing and some miles of level walking. You will do most of your climbing at the beginning regardless of your direction of travel, thus making the rest of the day more pleasant. EAST—Go N from the Galehead Hut the short distance to the trail intersection, and go R (SE) on the Twinway Trail which dips to a slight sag and then climbs steeply on a rocky trail to the bare summit of South Twin (4926 ft, 0.9 mi from the hut), where there are views in all directions. Here North Twin Spur goes L. You go R (S) on Twinway, descend a short distance to a broad ridge connecting South Twin and Guyot and follow a level path through young fir and balsam (a fire destroyed the forest here some years ago). In about 2.0 mi you will climb gently to the bare flat summit of Mt Guyot (4589 ft). Just before the summit at 3.0 mi, the Bondcliff Trail goes S (R), but you go E (L) up and over Guyot. The summit is partly covered with Krummholz (a mat of stunted trees a few feet high), and the rest is bare gravel dotted with the rare tundra plant Diapensia. It is a popular place to lunch on good days, but please sit on the gravel rather than the soft pincushion plants invitingly scattered about. They are easily destroyed by even the softest bottoms.

From Guyot the trail goes gently downhill on a NE ridge to a sag at 3.9 mi and ascends steeply to a knob in another 0.2 mi (good views). Now you move along the Zealand Ridge. At 5.0 mi a view opens R revealing Zeacliff Pond far below. The trail descends to the junction with the Zealand Trail (R) at 5.6 mi. Here there is a short side trail to an airy cliff overlooking Zealand Notch, well worth the short digression. Notice the trail far below, cut into the scree slope on the opposite side of the Notch (Ethan Pond Trail). From the trail intersection go L (N) on the Twinway Trail for a steep 1.5 mi descent through a birch forest. Cross Whitehall Brook at 6.8 mi; just beyond, the Lend-a-Hand Trail goes L to Mt Hale. Follow the brook R a short distance down to Zealand Falls Hut.
WEST—The Twinway Trail leads from behind the Zealand Hut. The mileage points are Zealand Cliff 1.4 mi; Mt Guyot 4.0 mi; South Twin Mt 6.1 mi.

4. ZEALAND FALLS—MIZPAH SPRING
8.0 mi (12.9 km) 2820 ft (860 m) E, 1800 ft (530 m) W
For a day with no views to speak of, we found this section most attractive because of its diversity and because of the cascades in the

brook that flows near Crawford Notch which are both beautiful and useful for bathing. From Zealand Falls Hut the trail skirts the edge of Zealand Pond, which has beaver dams and outlets at both ends, climbs easily through a boggy area recovering from past lumbering and goes steeply over a col between Mt Tom and Mt Field to Crawford Notch. From here it goes up the historic Crawford Path and Mizpah Cutoff to the Hilton of the high huts, Mizpah Spring Hut.

We passed a small group of young men and women expertly cutting, dressing and installing log walks over the worst of the bogs on the trail; we admired their axe work, commiserated with them over the black flies and mosquitoes that luxuriated in the bogs and thanked them for their work on the trails. This important job is paid for largely from the dues of the AMC. (You might wish to join the AMC and/or help financially in this effort; see address at beginning of Walk.) The work is for your benefit but not principally for your immediate ease. Its main purpose is to retard the erosion that can make these trails almost impassable and to save the fragile vegetation along them for everyone to enjoy. You will see evidence of trail crew work in many places—the log walkways, the waterbars to divert rainwater from the path, the great stone steps on steep slopes to reduce erosion and aid you on your way and the bridges across the larger streams. It all adds up to increase your enjoyment, and both verbal and monetary thanks are quite in order.

The footing is fair to good, the way well signposted but infrequently blazed. The routing, as described below, may be confusing in print since you are on part or all of six named trails. However, the signposts are a great help and generally include the direction and distance to the next hut. If you keep your map handy, it will help unravel the complex routing.

EAST—Leave Zealand Falls Hut from its N corner and go downhill, passing between two ponds, to a trail junction. The Ethan Pond Trail goes R (S) and the Zealand and A-Z trails go L (N) together. Take the latter and skirt Zealand Pond to a second junction where the A-Z Trail goes R (E) while the Zealand Trail continues ahead. Go R and begin to pick up blue blazes. You will pass through a boggy area with many log walks and cross two logging roads, remains of logging operations of several years ago. Beyond the second logging road you enter a mature deciduous forest, and the trail climbs steeply to the col between Mt Tom and Mt Field at 3.2 mi. Here the Willey Range Trail goes R (S). Shortly beyond, the Mt Tom Spur goes L about 0.8 mi to Mt Tom (4047 ft). Continue ahead (E); you begin to descend steadily and at times steeply into Crawford Notch.

At 4.1 mi you join the Avalon Trail, which comes in from the R; the descent soon eases as you parallel and then cross a sparkling brook running over smooth rock. Two cascades of this brook are remarkable enough to name—Beecher Cascade (where the trail crosses) and Pearl Cascade (signposted). Beyond Beecher Cascade the trail becomes an old woods road that leads you easily down to Crawford Notch just by the old railroad depot (now an AMC Information Center). Rt 302 is just beyond. Go L (N) on this road past the AMC Crawford Hostel (refreshments available here). Just before the historic Crawford House (circa 1859) now standing empty, go R (E) on the Crawford Path. Claimed to be the oldest continuously used mountain trail in the U.S., Crawford Path was cleared as a footpath in 1819 and converted to a bridle trail in 1840. It was made to carry people to the top of Mt Washington from the Crawford House.

In 0.4 mi from Rt 302 you enter national forest lands and reach the Gibbs Brook Scenic Area, a stand of virgin spruce and birch (the unseen brook can be heard on your L). The trail climbs steadily to the Mizpah Cutoff (7.3 mi from Zealand Falls and 1.8 mi from Rt 302). Go R on the Cutoff for 0.8 mi as it climbs steadily at an easy grade over a ridge and descends a short distance to Mizpah Spring Hut.

WEST—Leave Mizpah Spring Hut from its W end, on the Mizpah Cutoff, and go 0.8 mi to its junction with the Crawford Path. Go L (W) on the Crawford Path to Rt 302 (2.5 mi). Jog L and pick up the Avalon Trail to the L of the old railroad depot. Go W on the Avalon Trail for 1.8 mi to the A-Z Trail, and take the latter R until it joins the Zealand Trail (7.5 mi). Go L 0.2 mi to the Ethan Pond Trail junction and R another 0.2 mi up to the Zealand Falls Hut.

hard at work

5. MIZPAH SPRING—LAKES OF THE CLOUD
4.7 mi (7.6 km)/1585 ft (480 m)

This is the easiest section of the seven-day hike, and if the weather is clear, it is one of the most rewarding for views. You will be above treeline most of the time on the great long ridge that runs south from below the summit cone of Mt Washington. The ridge is dotted with three successively higher mountain peaks, stepping stones to the centerpiece of Mt Washington. Since the ridge itself is high, all the peaks are reached with little climbing.

You will meet more climbers in the summer on the Presidentials than you will in any of our other Walks, and the closer you get to that people-magnet, Mt Washington, the more you meet. If you are sociably inclined, you can spend the day between Mizpah and the Lakes huts stopping to talk to hikers. It paid off for one small lad. We stopped to chat with a father and three youngsters who were bound for Mizpah to spend the night. After exchanging pleasantries and admiring the chidren's packs and their sturdiness in carrying them, we parted. Not a mile farther on, we found a pair of neatly pressed small trousers lying in the trail. We scooped them up and accosted the next pilgrim going to Mizpah, who gladly undertook to deliver them to their young owner. The way is well cairned and the footing is good. In the case of severe weather, if you are at Mt Monroe, head for the Lakes Hut; if you are south of Monroe, retreat to Mizpah, avoiding the Loop Trail over Mt Eisenhower.

EAST—From the W end of Mizpah Spring Hut take the white-blazed Webster Cliff Trail N steeply uphill in woods for 0.5 mi to the flat open S summit of Mt Clinton (your first view of Mt Washington and of the humps of mountain peaks strung out along the ridge). Reenter woods to reach the open main summit (4275 ft). Mt Clinton was renamed Mt Pierce for the state's native-born president by the New Hampshire legislature, but the name just doesn't seem to stick. Shortly beyond the summit you rejoin the Crawford Path, coming in from the L, 0.8 mi from Mizpah. The trail dips slightly, and you pass a spring at 1.5 mi. At 1.9 mi you reach the Mt Eisenhower Loop, diverging L, to climb over Mt Eisenhower (4761 ft); renamed from Mt Pleasant, this new name has stuck. In good weather it is well worth the climb for the added view. The Crawford Path is safer in bad weather, however, as it slabs the SE side of Mt Eisenhower.

At 2.6 mi the Edmunds Path comes in from the L, and just beyond the Mt Eisenhower Trail (not to be confused with the Loop

Trail) goes R, leading down into Oakes Gulf and Dry River. There is a stagnant bit of water called Red Pond in the col NE of Mt Eisenhower and a good spring 0.2 mi beyond. From the spring you ascend fairly steeply to the summit of Mt Franklin (5004 ft, 3.2 mi). To the R an impressive precipice plunges down into Oakes Gulf. At 3.9 mi you reach the Mt Monroe Loop Trail which goes L, climbs the two summits of Mt Monroe (5385 ft) and rejoins the Crawford Path in 0.8 mi. If you stay on the Crawford Path, which goes R around a broad flat shoulder of Monroe, you will pass the Dry River Trail (R) at 4.4 mi.

As you round Monroe you will see the two Lakes of the Cloud and the hut ahead (the Crawford Path may be relocated from this shoulder, because of the fragile plants here).

WEST—From Lakes of the Cloud Hut take the Crawford Path W to the Webster Cliff Trail and the latter to the Mizpah Spring Hut. The mileages are Mt Monroe Loop Trail R 0.1 mi; Dry River Trail L 0.3 mi; other end of the Monroe Loop Trail R 0.8 mi; Edmunds Path R 2.1 mi; Mt Eisenhower Trail 2.1 mi; Mt Eisenhower Loop Trail R 2.2 mi; Webster Cliff Trail L 3.9 mi; Mt Clinton 4.0 mi.

a lake in the clouds

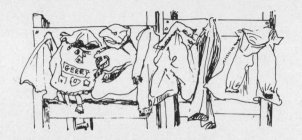

6. LAKES OF THE CLOUD—MADISON

7.3 mi (11.8 km)/3000 ft (790 m)

This section covers the mountain-studded ridge between Mt Washington and Mt Madison, with the Great Gulf yawning to the east and a series of ridges to the west. You will be above treeline all day and may go over or around, as you prefer, four peaks over 5500 feet, including Mt Washington, the highest peak in the Northeast. In reasonable weather it is an easy hike, especially if you avoid climbing all the peaks; and in clear weather, the views are unmatched anywhere east of the Rockies. We must add that in bad weather (high winds, low temperatures) this section can be dangerous; and we append the escape routes suggested by the AMC. The speed at which severe weather can set in and its severity are unbelievable unless you have already experienced it. A personal story will help illustrate the point. Years ago our family, intent on treating ourselves to a night at the Lakes Hut, toiled out of the Great Gulf. It was a blistering August day as we clambered over the lip of the Gulf and started up the short and not very steep slope to the summit of Mt Washington to reach the Crawford Path. The wind began to pick up, the sky clouded and sleet began to pummel us five minutes after we left the lip of the Gulf. On went all our sweaters, windbreakers, hats and gloves. Alas, however, our long pants were safely back at the Great Gulf Shelter and our bare legs were being unmercifully stung by the driving sleet. Progress slowed to a snail's pace and the youngest collapsed and had to be carried. Finally, nearly exhausted, we staggered into the safety of the Summit House. The happy ending was that we spent the night there (it was still a hotel). The next day in calm sunshine we proceeded to the Lakes Hut and returned in warm rain the following day to the Great Gulf. It was our closest approach to family disaster, and it was a lesson we parents never forgot. Clearly, we should have turned back at once when the bad weather hit.

There is little danger from just the frequent mist, however. The Crawford Path and Gulfside Trail are lined with cairns, with the top stones painted a bright yellow. The cairn spacing is such that, even in the densest mist, you will be able to see the next cairn ahead from the previous one.

You will cross the Mt Washington Railroad, a cog line that has been taking visitors to the top of Mt Washington since 1869. On a calm day its plume of black smoke is visible for miles and its puffing audible well beyond the Lakes Hut.

If you climb over Mt Washington rather than bypass it (and once, we suppose, is a must), remember that the summit is reached by both the auto road and the railroad and is a busy, noisy, crowded place in the summer.

NORTH—Leave the Lakes of the Cloud Hut from its N end by the Crawford Path, pass between the two small lakes and climb the W side of Mt Washington. At 0.8 mi the Davis Path comes in from the R, and shortly beyond the Westside Trail goes L. If you want to skip the summit of Mt Washington, thereby eliminating 700 feet of climbing and about a mile distance, go L on the Westside Trail. You will teeter over big boulders for 0.8 mi along the 5500 feet contour, pass under the cog railroad and immediately beyond join the Gulfside Trail 1.6 mi from the Lakes Hut. If you are climbing Mt Washington, continue ahead on the Crawford Path up the steep cone to the summit at 1.5 mi. Just before the summit by an old stone corral you pass the Gulfside Trail. Return to this spot from the summit and go R (N); in about 0.5 mi you will cross the cog railroad.

Beyond, the Great Gulf Trail goes straight ahead and the Gulfside Trail turns sharply L. Keep on the Gulfside Trail; in about 0.5 mi the Westside Trail comes in on the L. At 2.6 mi, in the Clay-Washington Col (5395 ft), the Mt Clay Loop Trail climbs R to Mt Clay (5532 ft). At 2.9 mi the Jewell Trail goes L (W). At 3.5 mi, in the Clay-Jefferson Col (4965 ft), a loop trail leads L to Greenough Spring (sure water). Shortly beyond, the Mt Clay Loop Trail rejoins the Gulfside Trail. Ascending gradually, you pass the Sphinx Trail (R) at 3.8 mi and The Cornice (trail) L at 4.2 mi. You are now on the Monticello Lawn, a relatively smooth, grassy plateau. The Jefferson Loop Trail leads L at 4.4 mi to the top of Mt Jefferson (5715 ft). The Gulfside Trail ascends around the E side of Jefferson, crosses Six Husbands Trail at 4.7 mi and descends to the

Edmunds Col (4930 ft), where there is an emergency refuge, a low quonset hut. Past the intersection with Randolph Path (5.0 mi) and beyond the col, ascend a narrow ridge between Castle Ravine (L) and Jefferson Ravine (R) with good views down into the latter. At 5.8 mi the Israel Ridge Path comes in L, briefly joins the Gulfside Trail and leads R at 6.2 mi to the summit of Mt Adams (5798 ft). The Gulfside Trail now goes over a grassy saddle between Mt Sam Adams (L) and Mt Adams (R).

Cross Lowe's Path at 6.4 mi at a point nicknamed "Thunderstorm Junction" and the Airline Trail at 6.9 mi. Both paths end at Mt Adams. From here you drop down to the Madison-Adams Col and the Madison Hut.

If the weather is fine when you pass between Mt Adams and Mt Sam Adams, or after dinner at Madison, we recommend a hike up Mt Adams. From the hut it is a mile round trip and a 540-ft climb. Not only are the views magnificent, but you will have bagged another 5000 footer. It is said that the peak is the location of spiritual energy similar to that claimed for Avebury and Stonehenge in Britain. A cult of this persuasion met on its summit a year or so ago and left some curious symbols on the rock.

SOUTH—The mileage points are Airline Trail 0.4 mi; Lowe's Path 0.9 mi; Israel Ridge Path 1.1 mi & 1.5 mi; Randolph Path 2.3 mi; Six Husbands Trail 2.6 mi; The Cornice (trail) 3.1 mi; Sphinx Trail 3.5 mi; Greenough Spring 3.8 mi; Westside Trail 4.8 mi; Mt Washington Summit 5.8 mi.

ESCAPE ROUTES—If caught by severe weather, you should get off the long exposed ridge of this section as soon as possible. Do not try to reach the buildings on the summit of Washington unless you are very close when bad weather strikes, since it will get rapidly worse the higher you go. If S of Mt Washington, descend to the Lakes Hut. If N, retreat into one of the ravines: use the Sphinx Trail or Six Husbands Trail to reach shelter in the Great Gulf (2.0 mi); the Randolph Path for the Log Cabin (2.0 mi); Lowe's Path to the Spur Trail for Crag Camp (about 1.0 mi); Castle Ravine Trail to the protection of Roof Rock (0.8 mi); or try the emergency refuge in Edmunds Col. If you find it impossible to reach any of these shelters, descend carefully without trail into any of the ravines and spend an uncomfortable night in the woods; exposure on the heights could prove fatal.

7. MADISON—PINKHAM NOTCH
6.1 mi (9.8 km)/2825 ft (864 m)
This section leaves the great ridge of the Presidentials, plunges

steeply over the Parapet into the Great Gulf and then follows easier grades to an old road which leads to the camp at Pinkham Notch. It is a fairly strenuous day in either direction. We chose the shortest and fastest way between hut and camp. We assume you will climb Mt Madison (5363 ft) after dinner while you are at the hut, but you could take the Osgood Trail from the hut over Mt Madison and rejoin our route at its lower end. This route is a mile longer, more exposed at its upper end and involves 500 feet of more climbing, but it has magnificent views. Do not attempt it in severe weather!

SOUTH—Take the Star Lake/Parapet Trail running S from Madison Hut. When the trails split go L on the Parapet Trail, passing E of Star Lake. At 0.3 mi go R on the Madison Gulf Trail and immediately begin descending steeply into the Great Gulf. You soon enter scrub, cross and recross a small brook and reach Mossy Slide at the foot of the headwall on the upper floor of the Gulf (0.8 mi). From here you descend more gradually to the lower floor, while passing the Sylvan Cascade, a handsome fall of water. Cross the lower floor and descend, sometimes steeply, to the Osgood Cutoff coming in L, 2.1 mi from the hut. Continue ahead (now with white blazes) and soon join the Great Gulf Trail on which you go R. Cross the W branch of the Peabody River, ascend its steep S bank and turn L back to the Madison Gulf Trail. At 4.0 mi a short trail leads L to Lowe's Bald Spot, a knob with a panoramic view of the northern peaks and the Carter-Moriah Range.

The Madison Gulf Trail continues with little change of elevation to the Mt Washington auto road at 4.1 mi. Go L (S) on the auto road, pass Nelson Crag Trail and the Raymond Path on R and just beyond turn R on the Old Jackson Rd (now a trail). At 5.5 mi, at the foot of a ski slalom slope, keep R. You join the Tuckerman Ravine Trail just before the Pinkham Notch Camp.

NORTH—Walk around the W end of the main building of the Pinkham Notch Camp (The Trading Post) to the Tuckerman Ravine Trail (a scale here to weigh your pack!). In just a few yds pick up the Old Jackson Rd going R, blazed white. The mileage points are Mt Washington auto road 1.8 mi (jog L on auto road 0.2 mi to Madison Gulf Trail R); Great Gulf Trail 3.9 mi (jog R on Great Gulf Trail back to Madison Gulf Trail), Osgood Cutoff 4.0 mi (leave white blazes) foot of Great Gulf headwall 5.7 mi, Parapet Trail 5.8 mi, Madison Hut 6.1 mi.

6a. LAKES OF THE CLOUD—PINKHAM NOTCH
4.5 mi (7.3 km)/3200 ft (976 m)

If you do a three-day circuit from Pinkham Notch or if you want to reduce the Walk by one day, you can eliminate the Madison Hut and go directly from the Lakes Hut to Pinkham Notch. The shortest route is by the Tuckerman Ravine Trail and Crossover. The former is the most popular trail in the White Mountains since it is also the shortest way to the summit of Mt Washington. It features the impressive glacial cirque of Tuckerman Ravine, with its towering headwall where the snow often lingers into late summer, and Hermit Lake, which affords a superlative vista of the Ravine and the encircling cliffs of Boott Spur and The Lion Head. The trail from Pinkham Notch to Hermit Lake is a wide, very rocky fire road about which the less said the better, but the steep climb up the headwall is worth every step of its steepness. You will also share the trail with many others. Be heartened if you are struggling; you are bound to be in better shape than some you'll meet.

EAST—From the N end of the Lakes Hut, three trails diverge. You take the middle one, the Tuckerman Crossover. It passes to the R of the lakes, rises gradually to the rocky, grassy Bigelow Lawn S of the cone of Mt Washington and drops down to Tuckerman Junction (0.9 mi) where a great cairn, resting pilgrims and a multiplicity of signs announce the meeting of five trails. You continue ahead (E) down to the lip of the headwall and pass in 200 yds the Alpine Garden Trail, which goes L. Continue down to and over the lip to a steep but good path that switchbacks down the headwall. Be careful not to dislodge stones which could put others in serious danger.

At the bottom of the steep pitch (1.4 mi) you may find the remnants of the great snowfield that fills the ravine in late winter and spring. Some years the melting snow forms a snow arch—do not walk under it, as people have been killed or injured by its collapse, but gaze at and photograph it from a respectful distance.

The bottom of the ravine is in two relatively level steps, with the intervening rise called the Little Headwall. Beyond this rise you reach at 2.1 mi the buildings of Hermit Lake (warden's cabin, a ski center manned by a helpful AMC employee and scattered open shelters). From here take the wide and uninteresting fire road 2.5 mi down to Pinkham Notch. Before you go, take a long last look back into the ravine from the sundeck of the ski center. It is the East's most Swiss-like scene. Just 0.4 mi before Pinkham there is a viewpoint of the Crystal Cascade of the Cutler River L a short distance off the fire road.

Note—From Tuckerman Junction there are two other routes down to Hermit Lake, dramatic trails along the descending arms that enclose the ravine. The Lion Head Trail (N from the junction) is the best known, with an "airy" drop down its precipitous end, but Boott Spur (S from the junction) keeps you above treeline longer. Tuckerman Ravine Trail is best in bad weather, however.

WEST—Leave from W end of the Trading Post of the Pinkham Notch Camp, and go out the Tuckerman Ravine Trail. The mileages are Hermit Lake 2.5 mi; snowfield (bottom of headwall) 3.1 mi; Tuckerman Junction 3.6 mi; Lakes of the Clouds 4.5 mi.

Lafayette

MANSFIELD WALK
Vermont, 4 days, 38.3 miles (61.8 km)

SECTION	DISTANCE		OVERNIGHT POINTS
1	7.1 mi	(11.5 km)	Jonesville-Bolton Valley
2	10.7 mi	(17.3 km)	Bolton Valley-Luce Hill
3	12.1 mi	(19.6 km)	Luce Hill-Mountain Road
4	8.4 mi	(13.5 km)	Mountain Road-Stowe

MAP—

USGS 7½-minute series: Richmond, VT (Sect 1), Bolton Mt, VT (Sects 1, 2 & 3), Mt Mansfield, VT (Sects 2 & 3), Hyde Park, VT (Sect 4). Order from: Branch of Distribution, US Geological Survey, 1200 S Eads Rd, Arlington, VA 22202.

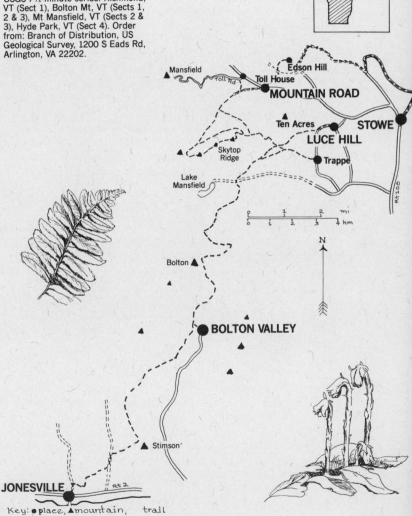

Key: ● place, ▲ mountain, trail

TRANSPORTATION
Jonesville—bus (Vermont Transit), Burlington & Boston or
Waterbury for bus (Greyhound) Burlington & NYC
or Waterbury for train (AMTRAK) NYC & Montreal
Stowe—bus (Vermont Transit) Waterbury 1 r/t dly for bus or
train as above

ACCOMMODATIONS (area code 802)
Bolton Valley, Bolton, VT 05477
  Bolton Valley Resort   434-2131
  Black Bear Lodge   434-2126

Luce Hill, Stowe, VT 05672
  Trapp Family Lodge   253-8511
  Ten Acres Lodge   253-7638

Mountain Road, Stowe, VT 05672
  The Inn on the Mountain   253-7311
  Ski Inn (Larry Heyer)   253-4050
  Fiddlers Green Inn   253-8124
  Edson Hill Manor   253-7371

This hike through the Mount Mansfield State Forest, from the
Winooski River north to the village of Stowe, is on the Long Trail
and cross-country ski trails. The route is exceptionally beautiful,
through varied evergreen and deciduous forests, with frequent
views of the surrounding mountains and distant farmlands. The
comfortable lodgings at the overnight points include the famous
Trapp Family Lodge near Stowe and the isolated but elegant
Bolton Valley Resort high on Bolton Mountain. Along the way you
will see the two best known Vermont peaks—Camel's Hump and
Mansfield.

41

The area has long been known for its resorts. In the late 1800s large frame hotels, serving Victorian city folk, were scattered in and around Stowe valley, with the bulk in the village itself. A hotel crowned Mt Mansfield and rustic camps in the deep woods catered to those who liked to rough it. Though the Victorian patrons are gone and so are the large hotels and the rustic camps, enough small country inns remain for those who prefer individuality and charm to the homogenized comfort of motels. The area is popular in winter as well as summer. Indeed, Mt Mansfield had the first ski chairlift in the country. In spite of its tourism, Stowe has kept its Vermont-village character, and the countryside away from the Mountain Road remains unspoiled, with well-tended farms in the valleys and unbroken forests stretching to the peaks.

Sometimes the countryside is best viewed from the dirt roads that give access to it, and we have therefore departed from our rule of as little road walking as possible by taking you the last day almost entirely by some of these little-changed back roads into Stowe village. There is not much auto traffic on them, and you will not only get magnificent vistas of the hills and mountains, but also more intimate sights of typical Vermont wooden barns, sugar houses and farmhouses. The way is so beautiful that we feel it should be signposted, "Danger, you are going through an area that may cause you to immigrate to Vermont."

The route is moderately strenuous, with poor to good footing, and should not be done by the completely inexperienced. It is not for travel while the snow lies in the high country (late November-late April).

Vermont patchwork

OVERNIGHT POINTS

Jonesville, on Rt 2, is just a post office crossroad kind of settlement surrounded by beautiful countryside. **Bolton Valley Resort** is a remote cluster of hotel and condominiums, open year-round, high at the head of uninhabited Bolton Valley. It is at the end of a five-mile access road and, while already at an elevation of 2000 feet, is surrounded by peaks on three sides. **Luce Hill** and the other remaining overnight points are all in the Stowe area. **Stowe** is an old Vermont village with all its traditional Vermont charms intact. Its only drawback is too many visitors at certain times of the year, but as we count ourselves among these, we can scarcely complain. May, June, September and October are the least busy times.

lunch

1. JONESVILLE—BOLTON VALLEY

7.1 mi (11.5 km)/2200 ft (670 m) N, 300 ft (90 m) S

This is a good leg-stretching start for the hike over the Mansfield Range. It is almost all on the Long Trail. You climb through woods from the miniscule village of Jonesville on the Winooski River to an isolated resort high in Bolton Valley, with the distinctive peak of Camel's Hump Mountain often in view. Although the trail goes through the woods much of the way and does not have a lengthy open ridge to traverse, your viewpoints are such that you do not need your topographic map to show you that you are going along a definite winding spine of land. It isn't often that a trail below treeline gives so many views of the contour of the land ahead, and we felt the trail under us as if we were flies walking on the curved backbone of a sleeping dragon which had the green earth in place of scales.

The way on the Long Trail is well marked and the footing good. You must be alert, however, to pick out the white trail markings when you are in one of the many groves of white birch.

NORTH—Just opposite the bridge over the Winooski River in Jonesville, a gravel road runs N from Rt 2 (white blazes are picked up immediately). Go about 0.5 mi up this road to a powerline crossing. The trail goes R off the road and follows the powerline for 0.2 mi before turning L into the woods. A short climb gains a rocky viewpoint for the Winooski Valley and the village of Jonesville below with the mountains beyond. From here you descend a short distance through beech woods, climb a rocky ridge, drop a short distance to a small stream and reach Duck Brook Shelter at 1.7 mi.

From the shelter follow an old woods road, becoming a trail along the W bank of Duck Brook, cross the brook on a wooden bridge and climb a narrow spine to the upper edge of a huge gravel pit at 1.9 mi (good views E). Follow edge of pit N back into the woods, past an unofficial campsite in a pine glade and up through a birch forest; cross a tributary of Duck Brook and then gravel Bolton Notch Road at 2.7 mi, and climb easily by paths and woods roads to a saddle. Turn L (N) and go over a series of small ridges to the indistinct summit of Stimson Mt at 3.5 mi. From here you descend, again over ridges, to Bolton Lodge (6.1 mi). The trail is well blazed but often not much in evidence underfoot.

Follow the blazes N from the Lodge to an old, once-graveled road, now a part of the Bolton Valley Resort X-C ski trail system. Go L (N) uphill on this road for 0.8 mi to a wide gravel road coming in from the R. You leave the Long Trail (LT) here (but will return to this point if continuing N the next day) and go R past a small pond to the Bolton Valley Resort (unmistakable when you see it because of its many buildings). Go R to the main parking lot and resort office. The Black Bear Lodge, a smaller place, is a short distance S on the paved access road.

SOUTH—From the main parking lot in front of the lodge follow signs to the X-C ski trails. When you reach the X-C Ski Center, go L (W) on a grassy gravel road past a small pond L to the beginning of the ski trail network and the intersection with the LT. Go L (SW) downhill on an old gravel road. White blazes are picked up here.

After a gentle 0.8 mi downhill a sign says "Trail's End," and a building appears ahead. Follow the white blazes off the gravel road past the building (Bolton Lodge), and go by an indistinct but well-blazed trail over Stimson Mt (3.6 mi) down to Bolton Notch Rd at 4.4 mi. Cross and enter a birch forest (blazes indistinct here), descend and cross a stream L, pass the edge of a huge gravel pit, descend to and cross Duck Brook and follow it downstream to Duck Brook Shelter (5.4 mi). Go R to a powerline (6.3 mi) and follow it R to a gravel road leading L into Jonesville.

Camel's Hump

2. BOLTON VALLEY—LUCE HILL
10.7 mi (17.3 km)/2170 ft (660 m)

This section is a cross-country ski trail across the east flank and spur of Bolton Mountain and the south slope of the valley leading to Nebraska Notch. It connects the Bolton Valley Resort with the extensive cross-country ski trails of the Trapp Family Lodge. The trail was laid out in 1970 by the cooperative effort of the Bolton Valley Resort, the Trapp Family Lodge and the State of Vermont and is now maintained by the Resort (our thanks to them all). The trail climbs high on Bolton Mountain on an old woods road built in the early 1900s, then through woods on a ski trail along the spur of Bolton Mountain and down the valley of the Michigan Brook to a woods road to Nebraska Notch. Another old woods road takes you to the Trapp Family Lodge ski trails.

The route over Bolton Mountain is in heavy evergreen forest, and there is a strong sense of remoteness much of the way. We attempted this section in early April, to be turned back by the still-heavy snow cover high on Bolton, and came back in June to summer verdure, a startling contrast to the snow. On the first struggle up, through the soft deep snow, we were arrested by the sight of large animal tracks crossing the trail. They were the distinctive round paw marks of the wildcat, larger than any we had ever seen and considerably fresher than we thought comfortable. As we bent over the tracks, a large branch crashed noisily to the ground just off the trail. Our hearts were in our mouths until it became evident that it was the wind which had broken the branch and not the weight of some steely clawed animal. We still maintain this had nothing to do with our turning back!

The way is well blazed and the trail well in evidence most of the way. There are three miles of trail on the spur of Bolton Mountain with no footpath, only a marked swath cleared of trees and shrubs, much overgrown with grasses and ferns in summer.

steely claws

NORTH—From the Bolton Valley Resort follow signs to the X-C ski trails. They lead past the X-C Ski Center and W downhill for 0.2 mi, past a small pond to a junction with the LT and the Bolton Mt Trail. Go R (N) on an old woods road, signposted to Bryant Lodge and Bolton Mt Trail. You will see four different blazes for the next few miles, the white oblong of the LT, blue blazes, small boards with white dots on them and *your* blazes, oblongs of red plastic. The road rises easily but steadily to the small Bryant Lodge (1.5 mi) and then continues through a fairly level, high valley, signposted "Heavenly Road"—a small relief from climbing. Soon, however, the LT goes L (W); you continue ahead on the old woods road, climbing steadily and somewhat more steeply along the E flank of Bolton Mt with views of the Waterbury Valley. The gradient eases, and at about 3.0 mi and 3300 ft elevation the route leaves the woods road and turns sharply R (E) and goes through the woods on a spur of Bolton Mt. There is no path underfoot for the next 3.0 mi, but the woods are naturally open enough for X-C skiing. The red plastic cards are well in evidence, high on the trees above the winter snows, and are set at reasonably close intervals. You should have no difficulty in holding to the route, but it will require a bit more care than following a well-trodden path. The route follows the spur for about a mile and offers great views down into the Cotton Brook basin and the Waterbury Reservoir SE and the Stowe Valley E. The trail swings gradually around as you cross the N side of the spur and descend into the Michigan Brook basin. You reach the brook in another mile or so and stay near it until you reach another woods road running down to Nebraska Notch auto road. The woods road passes a small rude cabin at 6.0 mi and reaches a clearing at 6.5 mi—unmistakably an old farm, with gnarled apple trees, the stone foundations of the farmhouse and tumbled stone walls going into the woods. In the next mile the woods road follows the Michigan Brook closely, and you will see numerous cascades and small waterfalls. In warm weather the pools below the cascades are perfect for cooling off.

At 7.5 mi you reach the gravel Nebraska Notch Rd. (Lake Mansfield is about 0.7 mi L, at the head of the valley.) Leave the blazes here. Go L on the road, crossing the Miller Brook (the stream running down from the Notch). Just beyond another gravel road goes R (N). Follow this road 0.7 mi to a clearing, house and pond. Continue ahead (E) on a much poorer road, the Old County Rd, which shortly passes another house. Continue E on an even poorer surface, cross a brook and go up a gully where the old road has been badly eroded. If in doubt here, the old road holds to the same direction as before. A small stream joins it for a brief distance, and you pass an old farm clearing (apple trees). Beyond the clearing you reach Russel Knoll, marked by signs, the limit of the Trapp Lodge ski trails. Take the Russel Knoll Trail R for about 1.5 mi to the Trapp Lodge. If you are staying at Ten Acres Lodge, continue on the Old County Rd to the paved Luce Hill Rd and go L to the lodge. The distance to Ten Acres is about 1.5 mi longer.

SOUTH—From the X-C Ski Center of the Trapp Lodge, walk NW on the main ski trail along the edge of the woods to Maria Plaza, pick up the Russel Knoll Trail and follow it to its end. Here a woods road (the Old County Rd), marked only "not patrolled," goes W downhill, turning into a good gravel road running down to Nebraska Notch.

If you are staying at Ten Acres Lodge, go uphill on Luce Hill Rd 0.5 mi to the Old County Rd and go R. The Russel Knoll Trail comes into the County Rd from the Trapp Lodge in about 1.5 mi; continue on the old road to the Nebraska Notch Rd. Go L on the latter across a bridge to a red-blazed woods road going R up Michigan Brook. Follow the red blazes for 7.2 mi to a junction with a wide gravel road running L to the Bolton Valley Resort.

the Hilton

3. LUCE HILL—MOUNTAIN ROAD
12.1 mi (19.6 km)/1200 ft (365 m)

In this section you spend the day on cross-country ski trails, so little used in the snowless months that you will be mostly in
solitude. It is a challenging day for pathfinding as there is no visible track underfoot, and you will have as close a sense of
bushwhacking (going across country off trails) as is possible and
yet still be guided by blazes. You leave Luce Hill by the Trapp
Lodge trails and connect with those of Mt Mansfield. If you are
staying the night at Edson Hill Manor, you will also use their ski
routes. At day's end you can enjoy the satisfaction gained from
crossing fairly uncharted country. Because the trails are kept free
only of trees and bushes, in late spring and summer you will be
walking, where the forest canopy is thin enough to let in the sun,
through a heavy growth of ferns and grasses. You will thus get
closely acquainted with these plants; in early morning or in rain
they will soak you to the waist. This is nice on hot days but not so
pleasant on cold ones.

The lack of a visible footpath will force you to be more dependent on the blazes. When none are in sight, the forest may look
the same in all directions. When this happens, remember the
general direction of the trail, as cross-country ski trails tend to be
straight lines in such circumstances; another blaze will be picked
up shortly. In most places, a narrow swath has been cleared of trees
and shrubs, leaving a green alley to watch for. But where the summer growth is lush, you cannot see the ground and progress is
necessarily slow, as your foot feels the way rather than your eye.
You can consider this section a challenge rather than trouble.

NORTH—From the Touring Center of the Trapp Family Lodge,
go W on well-kept ski trails and follow the sign to the Cabin. The
recommended summer route from the Lodge is Sugar Rd to the
Picnic Knoll and then the Owl's Hoot Trail to the Cabin. The latter trail is not well marked near the Cabin but is mostly on an old
woods road going NW uphill.

If you are staying at Ten Acres Lodge, go up Luce Hill Rd about
0.5 mi to the Old County Rd and take it R. It is passable by auto
for a mile, but soon deteriorates into a badly eroded gully.
Another road goes R to avoid this bit and soon joins the main
route. Continue ahead on the old road until you reach the
signposted Owl's Hoot Trail crossing from the Trapp Lodge. Go R
to the Cabin. From here you get a good view of the S end of Mt
Mansfield.

From the Cabin (3.1 mi from the Trapp Lodge), take the Haul Rd. What used to be called the Little Meadow is now the shambles left by clear cutting. You have two choices of routes from here to the Ranch Valley (a third if you are very strong). You can go by the Underhill and Burt trails (Luce Hill-Mountain Rd 12.1 mi) or by the shorter Ranch Camp Trail (7.7 mi). The third way is via the Skytop and Burt trails over three small peaks (13.1 mi). These routes are little used even in winter, and it was about them we addressed our caveats. The shortest route is also the easiest underfoot. The longest route has the added difficulty of fairly steep climbs and descents. If you are staying at a lodging on the Mountain Rd (Rt 108), we recommend the Underhill route as giving a day's hike of some challenge, and this is the one we describe fully. If you elect to stay at Edson Hill Manor you may want to take the shorter Ranch Camp Trail as the Manor is 1.5 mi beyond the Mountain Rd.

In 1981 the start of the Underhill and Skytop trails was hard to find because of recent lumbering. The safest way is to watch for a lonely signpost on the Haul Rd at the edge of the cut-over wasteland, about 0.5 mi from the Cabin. This sign is for the Ranch Camp Trail (not described here but fairly straightforward and well marked to the Camp). For the others, from the sign go L (W) uphill along the forest edge for perhaps 0.2 mi and watch closely for other signs. You will finally spy on two trees one marking a saddle (Rob George Saddle, once a dim cathedral of large pines), the other marking the Underhill and Skytop trails, which stay together for awhile. All these trails are blazed by the same type of red plastic squares used on the Bolton Mt Trail.

When the joined Underhill and Skytop trails split, the junction is signposted; Skytop goes L uphill. We have only walked Skytop for 0.5 mi, long enough to assure ourselves that it was similar to the Underhill Trail except steeper and with blazes somewhat farther apart. Unless you are going on to Edson Hill Manor, we recommend the Underhill Trail. You will have 3.0 mi of fairly level but heavy going along the N side of the Skytop Ridge. Take it slowly, and enjoy the ferns and their myriad companions. You will cross many small streams, all safe to drink from. Occasionally you will follow a woods road, a relief from the slant of the hillside. The junction with the Burt Trail cannot be missed, a small worry we had since the Underhill Trail continues on to the LT. The signposted Burt Trail comes downhill from the L just before a large stream. Cross the stream to a second signposted junction, and take the Burt Trail R (the Underhill Trail continues ahead). The footing is immediately easier because you are going downhill, and it steadily improves as the path becomes a woods road. The road follows the stream you crossed until you reach the Ranch Brook.

The Ranch Camp Trail comes in from the R near the ruins of the Ranch Camp. Here you cross the brook and follow its N bank to the paved Mountain Rd. If you are inclined for a swim, the brook has many crystal pools, some quite secluded from the trail. If you are staying at the Inn on the Mountain, before you reach the paved road take a X-C ski trail L marked "Crosscut," which will take you to the Mt Mansfield X-C Ski Center. A trail leads uphill from the center a short distance through the woods to the bottom of the Mt Mansfield Toll Rd and the Inn. If you are going to one of the lodgings located on the Mountain Rd, follow the Ranch Camp Rd out to the paved Mountain Rd (Rt 108). Ski Inn and Fiddlers Green Inn are a short distance R on Rt 108.

Mansfield

For Edson Hill Manor go R (S) on the Mountain Rd past Stowe School, and take the first gravel road L. After it bends round N look carefully on the trees R for a round red metal marker. It marks a narrow ski-touring path going E. Take this path, twice crossing a stream on logs (markers hard to find after second bridge), until you come to an open field. Walk NE diagonally across the field to a gravel road. Go L on this road to a private driveway marked "Hankinson," and take a grassy path R (before the driveway) into woods (red marker). Soon you'll reach another field with a white house. Go R along the edge of the woods to an old woods road, and go L. You soon emerge onto a gravel road with a sign to Edson Hill Manor and Top Notch. Go L uphill to a broad path R with a sign indicating "Stehl" just inside the woods. Take this path, and in a few minutes go R on a woods road which leads down to the Edson Hill Manor gravel access road by their trout pond. Go L to the Manor.

screech owl

SOUTH—From Edson Hill Manor walk out the access road past the trout pond. Just beyond, go R on a woods road marked with red plastic markers. Follow this road for a short distance to an intersection, and go L (W) another short distance to a gravel road. Go L to the bend where a sign lists Edson Hill Manor and Topnotch. Turn R off the gravel road on what looks like an old lane (not marked). In a short distance take a path R leading to the corner of an open field with a white house ahead R and a woods L. Follow the border of the woods to a path L (round red markers), and follow it to a gravel road. Jog L (sign here for Hankinson (driveway), climb a bank and cut across an open field to the SW corner, where markers lead through woods to another gravel road. Turn L and go steeply down to the Mountain Rd (Rt 108). Go R to the first road L after the Ski Inn, the Ranch Camp Rd.

From the Inn on the Mountain, walk from the bottom of the Toll Rd by a path S a short distance to the Mt Mansfield Ski Center. Take the Crosscut Trail to the Ranch Camp Rd, and go R. Take either the Ranch Camp Trail L or continue on the dirt road, which becomes the Burt Trail, to the Underhill Trail and go L. Both the Underhill Trail and the Ranch Camp Trail end at a lumbered area which you cross to the Haul Rd. Go R to the Cabin and take the Owl Hoot Trail down to the Old County Rd.

If going to the Trapp Family Lodge, continue across the Old County Rd and follow signs to the Lodge. For Ten Acres Lodge, go L on Old County Rd to the paved Luce Hill Rd, and turn L.

4. MOUNTAIN ROAD—STOWE
8.4 mi (13.5 km) / 700 ft (210 m)
The way we have chosen from the Mountain Road to the village of Stowe is an exception to our rule of taking you on off-road routes. We picked this section as a prime example of the old-fashioned dirt country roads which still exist in northern Vermont. We feel that you have not truly seen the countryside without an excursion along them. Most of the way is along these roads, and except at the height of summer, you will share them with few cars, generally local ones who courteously drive slowly past you. The views from these roads are the equal of those you get along the trails. You will gain more intimate glimpses into the farms through which you pass, and you will have a fine view of Stowe nestling in the valley below. You will have fine views from Stowe Valley of the long, bare ridge of Mt Mansfield.

EAST—Follow the directions in Section 3 for getting from the Mountain Rd to Edson Hill Manor until you reach the second gravel road. Go R 0.5 mi to its junction with the gravel Edson Hill Rd, and then go L. In 0.2 mi you pass the entrance to Edson Hill Manor, from which you would come if staying there (1.7 mi from the Mountain Rd). Continue to a fork, and go R (Weekshill Rd). In 2.8 mi you come to Percy's Farm and a fork in the road; take the L fork, a sharp turn uphill between the house and barn, on Percy Rd. There are post-card views of Stowe village below. Go up Percy Rd for 0.6 mi to a fork and turn R (West Hill Rd). Keep on this road, bending R at 0.3 mi down to Rt 100 at the Grand Union Market (7.5 mi from the Mountain Rd, 5.8 mi from Edson Hill Manor). Go R on Rt 100 through the center of Stowe village 0.8 mi to the bus stop at Stowe Quick Mart. Waterbury is 10.0 S on Rt 100; a taxi would help take advantage of the more frequent transportation service there.

WEST—Walk N on Rt 100 from the bus stop through Stowe village, and take a road L by the Grand Union Market, 0.8 mi from the bus stop. This road climbs out of the valley and ends at another road. Here go L downhill 0.6 mi through Percy's Farm, and take a sharp R fork for 2.8 mi to another fork L. The entrance to Edson Hill Manor is 0.2 mi from this fork. If you are staying on the Mountain Rd, continue past this entrance to a gravel road R, turn and go R 0.5 mi. Look on a tree L for a sign indicating Top Notch L and Edson Hill Manor R. Here you leave the gravel road on an old lane L and follow the trail description of Section 3 SOUTH.

Stowe Village

SHERBURNE WALK
Vermont, 4 days, 43.8 miles (70.6 km)

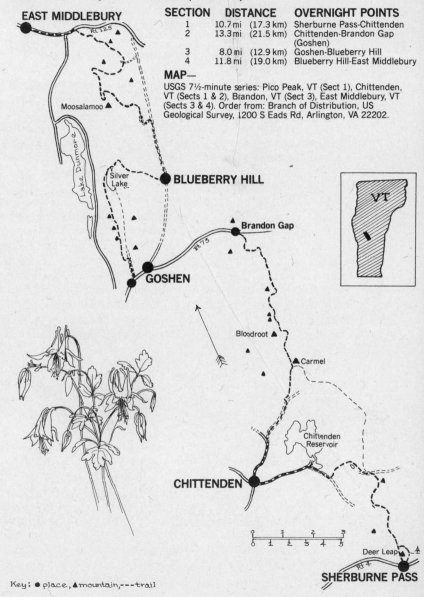

SECTION	DISTANCE		OVERNIGHT POINTS
1	10.7 mi	(17.3 km)	Sherburne Pass-Chittenden
2	13.3 mi	(21.5 km)	Chittenden-Brandon Gap (Goshen)
3	8.0 mi	(12.9 km)	Goshen-Blueberry Hill
4	11.8 mi	(19.0 km)	Blueberry Hill-East Middlebury

MAP—

USGS 7½-minute series: Pico Peak, VT (Sect 1), Chittenden, VT (Sects 1 & 2), Brandon, VT (Sect 3), East Middlebury, VT (Sects 3 & 4). Order from: Branch of Distribution, US Geological Survey, 1200 S Eads Rd, Arlington, VA 22202.

EAST MIDDLEBURY

Rt 125

Moosalamoo

Lake Dunmore

Silver Lake

BLUEBERRY HILL

Brandon Gap

Rt 73

GOSHEN

VT

Bloodroot

Carmel

Chittenden Reservoir

CHITTENDEN

Deer Leap

Rt 4

SHERBURNE PASS

Key: ● place, ▲ mountain, --- trail

54

TRANSPORTATION
Sherburne Pass—bus (Vermont Transit) Rutland 2 r/t dly
Middlebury—bus (Vermont Transit) Pittsfield & Rutland

ACCOMMODATIONS (area code 802)
Sherburne Pass, Killington, VT 05751
    The Inn at Long Trail   775-7181
    Mountain Meadows Lodge   755-1010

Chittenden, VT 05737
    Tulip Tree Inn   483-6213

Brandon, VT 05733
    Churchill House Inn   247-3300

Goshen, VT 05733
    Blueberry Hill Inn   247-6735

East Middlebury, VT 05740
    Wayberry Inn   388-4015

For reservations at the inns listed (except The Inn at Long Trail and Wayberry Inn) call or write Churchill House Inn and mention this book. These inns are part of the Vermont hike—inn to inn scheme (described p 56).

This Walk in central Vermont is partly on the Long Trail and partly on side trails that parallel it. There are not the vistas that other sections offer, but the woods are rich in nature's bounty, with a wealth of plants and flowers for eager amateur botanists to identify. Parts of the trail come out on open meadows or country roads offering glimpses of red barns and other buildings nestling in the open hillsides that penetrate the wooded mountains. These views retain a uniquely Vermont look, which we find difficult to characterize. Surely there is a special aura about the Vermont countryside.

The Walk is noted for the individuality and unfailing high quality of the inns that offer hospitality along the way. Here in this part of Vermont we have found a group of innkeepers who have cooperatively worked out inn-to-inn hiking tours. Hikers are therefore especially welcomed. They go further than we have visualized by picking you up from your point of arrival and delivering you to your trailhead and vice versa if you wish, to eliminate road walking. They also furnish you with the latest changes in the trail routing and, all in all, couldn't be more helpful. You even can make one point of contact for most of the accommodations for the whole Walk (Churchill House Inn), thus saving you the trouble of contacting each inn.

OVERNIGHT POINTS

Sherburne Pass is a saddle in the long spine of the Green Mountains 10 mi east of Rutland on Rt 4. It contains only the road, the Long Trail crossing and the Inn at Long Trail. **Chittenden** is a tiny village well off the main roads. The site sits dreaming around a handsome statue of a Civil War soldier, a monument to local men who served in that war. One wonders where all the lads commemorated by the statue came from in so sparsely settled a region. **Goshen** is even smaller and less compact than Chittenden and is equally remote. **Blueberry Hill** is the comfortable inn of that name on a back dirt road. **East Middlebury** is a larger village on the outskirts of Middlebury, two miles from Rt 7. It is astride the Middlebury River and has in it many attractive colonial wooden buildings, a pleasant living village to walk around and explore.

cardinal

1. SHERBURNE PASS—CHITTENDEN
10.7 mi (17.3 km) / 1630 ft (497 m)

This section is an easy walk through woods with only moderate climbs. You pass by two shelters, one especially well sited by a clear running stream, and go along one end of a high sheet of water (in New England called a pond rather than a lake), with the tiny Vermont village of Chittenden marking the end of your hike.

window
in the
tunnel

There are few views unless you take the Deer Leap Trail loop, a steep, rocky climb with much scrambling. There is a little cave near the beginning from which emerges a constant draft of cool air, very refreshing on a hot day. Only if you are a novice to rock scrambling or the day is poor should you go by the Long Trail in this area. At the Chittenden end the variety of woods through which you pass, the lush foliage underneath as well as the country-side which opens up before you provide the interests of the day. The location of a place as attractive as the Inn at Long Trail right at the trailhead in Sherburne Pass is another bonus.

NORTH—From the trailhead in Sherburne Pass on Rt 4 (just E of the Inn at Long Trail), climb steeply N on a white-blazed trail, here jointly the Appalachian Trail (AT) and the Long Trail (LT). Almost immediately there is a fork, with the blue-blazed Deer Leap Trail loop going L and the AT/LT going R. The loop, which we prefer, is the same distance as the LT, but is more strenuous. After climbing precipitously over rocks, affording some breath-taking views, it offers a pleasant interlude through a stand of evergreens and birches, with a particularly thick and beautiful ground cover of wood sorrel and ferns. The loop ends with a rocky descent around an impressive outcrop and an easy climb to rejoin the LT, 1.3 mi from the pass. If you take the LT from the pass, the blue-blazed AT goes R in 0.5 mi and the white-blazed LT L, the latter meeting the Deer Leap loop at 1.3 mi.

Shortly past the loop junction bear R and travel along a pleasant easy path, descending gently. At 1.8 mi you reach Johnson Shelter. If you are walking when the trees are leafless you will get some views, but in summer only tantalizing hints appear through the leaves. At 3.0 mi you pass a sign pointing ahead 3.0 mi to South Pond Trail; cross a dirt road with Elbow Rd marked to R and come to a yellow arrow pointing you uphill to avoid wet spots in the old trail. At 5.4 mi you reach Rolston Rest Shelter, beside a clear bubbling brook. The path continues to a dirt road (5.8 mi) on which you turn L (W), leaving the LT. There are *no* blazes along this road, and when you come to its end near Noyes (South) Pond, you must look sharply L for blue blazes leading you beside the pond on a narrow trail and across its outlet at the N end. From here it is a steep, narrow descent on good footing. When the grade lessens and you come to a fork, keep R. You will find yourself on an old woods road, now overgrown and wet in places, that leads to the old dirt Chittenden-Pittsfield Rd (7.8 mi). Go R 1.5 mi to a paved road running L down to Chittenden. The Tulip Tree Inn is 0.5 mi before Chittenden, on R.

SOUTH—Walk E from the Tulip Tree Inn 0.5 mi, past a huge water pipe; 0.3 mi beyond, go R on a gravel road. At 2.9 mi from Chittenden you will see on the L a blue-blazed trail with a chain across. Follow this trail up to and around the outlet of Noyes (South) Pond to a dirt road. Go R (E, no blazes) until the white-blazed LT crosses (4.9 mi); go R here. The blue-blazed Deer Leap Trail loop goes off R at 9.4 mi, rejoining the LT just before Rt 4. The AT joins the LT from the L 0.5 mi before Rt 4, if you do not take the loop trail.

Horrid Cliffs

2. CHITTENDEN-BRANDON GAP
13.3 mi (21.5 km)/1950 ft (595 m)

There are not many views on this hike, so you can concentrate on getting more closely acquainted with the Vermont forest ground cover. In the growing season there will be a progression of plants. Uncovered by the melting snow in early spring are the still-green mosses, ground pines, Christmas ferns and partridge berry runners. It takes but little warming to usher in that profusion of bloom that later makes spring the hiker's paradise—hosts of delicate spring beauty, violet, bloodroot and trout lily, to mention only a few of the more common varieties. Summer will bring wood sorrel among the fully feathered ferns, while in autumn the hiker will see that the dwarf cornel has replaced its spring dress of white-flower crosses with its winter garb of red-berry clusters over circles of green petal leaves, thereby earning its other name of bunchberry.

Bunch Berry

The hike goes out a dead-end gravel road to an old woods road that now leads up to but once led over the long main ridge of the Green Mountains. At the top the road meets the Long Trail where, in the next few miles, you are introduced to the worst and the best of the normal Long Trail footing—worst in a two-mile tangle of roots, bogs and rocks, and best in a five-mile section of smooth, gently graded old woods road. In summer there are infrequent glimpses of far views and a few clear windows to the outside world, but this shady, cool and remote section of the Long Trail earns its nickname, "The Long Green Tunnel." Near Brandon Gap you get good views of the Horrid Cliffs, the rocky face of the north side of the gap. The name is a bit much for a modestly beetling cliff.

You will be spending the night at the Churchill House Inn near Goshen. We have planned that you will not hike the four miles from Brandon Gap to the inn, as the kind proprietors of Churchill House have agreed to pick you up at Brandon Gap if coming north or drop you off there if coming south.

NORTH—After saluting the statue in Chittenden, the quiet figure in forage cap gazing S at distant and long-ago battles, take the paved road N. If coming from the Tulip Tree Inn, go W 0.5 mi to the first intersection and R over the bridge, past the statue and straight ahead. The pavement ends just beyond the Mountain Top Inn, 1.9 mi from the statue. Continue ahead on a deserted gravel road, marked "dead-end," until you reach an old woods road going L, the New Boston Trail, 3.7 mi from Chittenden. (It is possible to shorten the hike by these miles if you avail yourself of the lift offered by the Tulip Tree Inn). The woods road is festooned with red and blue plastic diamonds marking ski trails, but don't let them lead you on. After leaving the gravel road a second woods road, marked "Carmel Camp," soon goes R, with faint blue painted blazes on top of the old axe-cut blazes. A few side roads go off, but you ascend easily and steadily NE on a well-trodden track. At 1.2 mi from the gravel road you pass a clearing with a few tent platforms from the old Carmel Camp, replaced in 1976 by the David Logan Shelter farther on. From here you climb 0.2

mi and join the LT 5.7 mi from Chittenden. The LT comes in so unobtrusively from the R (S) that only the sign "New Boston Trail," pointing back the way you came, will alert you.

The faint blue blazes are now replaced by equally faint white blazes (in 1981), but the way is highly visible underfoot and every side trail is signposted. From the junction climb up and over a shoulder of Mt Carmel and descend to Wetmore Gap (6.6 mi) along the W side of the ridge; views W emphasize the steepness of the ridge here. From the gap climb to and along the E side of the ridge on a poor trail, all rocks, roots and mud. Just as you are wondering why you have come, you hit a gentle and easy woods road. Pass Bloodroot Gap at 9.1 mi, Chittenden Brook Trail at 11.3 mi and reach Brandon Gap and Rt 73 at 13.3 mi. Churchill House Inn is 4 mi to the L.

SOUTH—At the height of land at Brandon Gap on Rt 73 go S on the white-blazed LT. The trailhead is just across the road from the parking lot situated out of sight well above the road. The mileages are Chittenden Brook Trail 2.0 mi; Bloodroot Gap 4.2 mi; Wetmore Gap 6.7 mi; New Boston Trail 7.6 mi; gravel road 9.6 mi.

3. GOSHEN—BLUEBERRY HILL
8.0 mi (12.9 km) / 830 ft (250 m)

This section takes you by a trail along a high ridge sandwiched between two lakes and by cross-country ski trails, from Churchill House Inn near Goshen to Blueberry Hill Inn standing alone in its own farmland. You start on a dirt road, climb wooded Sandler Ridge between Lake Dunmore and Silver Lake, descend to and skirt the shore of isolated Silver Lake, gleaming like its name when the sun shines, and go by the cross-country ski trails of the Blueberry Inn to the inn itself.

When we passed a meadow near the start of the trail, we noticed a marsh hawk swooping buoyantly over the far corner. Suddenly a flight of smaller birds mobbed him noisily. To escape their harassment, he flew directly toward us at head level, swerved at the last moment and disappeared into the woods. Both hawk and humans were surprised at this close encounter, and we were thrilled to see him so near. This and the walk along the shores of Silver Lake were the highlights of the day for us.

The footing is good to excellent except for a short, wet part beyond the lake. The route is well marked throughout.

NORTH—From the Churchill Inn walk N on Rt 73 a short distance to the first dirt road L. Go out the dirt road past an attrac-

marsh hawk

tive grey frame house and a ski trail R, signposted ''The Goat,''
over a bridge to a fork. Go R to a second fork and L at this fork,
over a second bridge; ignore a blue-blazed trail R marked
''Switchback,'' and go over a third bridge 1.0 mi from Rt 73. Trail
signs indicate that straight ahead is the Leicester Hollow Trail and
L is the Sandler Ridge Trail. Take the L trail, and climb steadily
and not too steeply to Sandler Ridge. (It is possible to use the
Leicester Hollow Trail, but we have not walked it.) The trail goes
up and down along this ridge and swings around the bumps it
doesn't go over. In about 3.0 mi you will see the shine of Lake
Dunmore through the trees to the L below you. In another mile
there is a small rock outcrop with a partial view of the lake.

You now cross to the E side of the ridge and descend to the
rocky shore of Silver Lake (5.0 mi from the Inn). It retains its wild
privacy because it can only be reached by shanks' mare (on foot),
and although it has some well-sited campsites on the far shore, we
found, even in mid-summer, that we had the lake to ourselves.
Walk N along its shore, through a fine evergreen forest mixed
with hardwoods, to the dam. You may want to pause here and explore the lake or take a dip. At the dam there are signs pointing
the way to Lake Dunmore and Mt Moosalamoo. Cross the dam
and follow the wire line E until you pick up blue markers and a
sign to Blueberry Hill on a dirt road. Take the L fork of this road
going uphill. Farther on avoid going L on trail at horseshoe bend;
follow blue blazes and diamonds. In 0.5 mi pick up a X-C ski trail
with numbered markers; the first is 10. Go L on this ski trail,
through woods and marshes, across a stream to a junction 8. Go R
and pass 6.

Soon the trail gives way to a gravel road at a house on your L.
Continue down this road until it ends by a farm at a wider, more
traveled gravel road. The inn is to the L.

trout lily

SOUTH—Go S on the gravel road in front of the Blueberry Inn to first dirt road R, and follow to its end; continue on a X-C ski trail past a blue 6 marker. At a junction 8 go L and follow trail past 10 R to a dirt road. Continue following blue markers to a powerline, and follow this line R (W) to Silver Lake. Cross the dam and go S along the W shore to the first blazed trail R (Sandler Ridge Trail). The trail climbs the ridge, follows it S for several miles and descends to a dirt road. Go R on this road to Rt 73 and again R to the Churchill House Inn.

4. BLUEBERRY HILL—EAST MIDDLEBURY
11.8 mi (19.0 km) / 1860 ft (565 m)
The centerpiece of this day's hike is a climb up a modest mountain with the improbable name of Moosalamoo (you soon find it rolling off your tongue). You leave Blueberry Hill by an untraveled gravel road, climb Mt Moosalamoo and go down its long north ridge to a wooded valley leading to East Middlebury. There are several viewpoints on Moosalamoo. You have a short bit of road walking into East Middlebury alongside a deep dramatic gorge. As you cross the lower part of this gorge on an old stone bridge, look over the side at a perfect old-fashioned country-style swimmin' hole. It is great for cooling off on a hot summer day, as the local children were demonstrating the day we passed. The way is generally easy to follow, with a few confusing bits; the footing is good to poor.
NORTH—Walk N from the Blueberry Inn on the quiet gravel road that runs in front of the inn. It is mostly through forest, but there is an occasional farm. At 2.2 mi you reach the Mooslamoo Campground Rd (signposted). Go L 0.5 mi to a small sign-in shelter. Opposite is a hand pump and the signposted Mt Moosalamoo Trail (blue blazed). This trail circles the campground, crosses the N branch of Voter Creek on a footbridge and climbs by an easy grade around the N and W side of Mt Moosalamoo. The way is well trodden by campers. You want to find a blue-blazed trail going R about 0.2 mi before the summit

(5.2 mi from the inn). As this trail was not signposted in June 1981, we missed it and arrived at the signposted summit of Mt Moosalamoo (2630 ft), so we had to backtrack. The side trail goes R into deep woods; the first and only viewpoint on Moosalamoo occurs shortly beyond this trail (so you know you have missed the side trail if you come to a viewpoint).

Once on the side trail, you will realize it is fairly new. It was laid out in 1979 and the stumps are still raw looking. Level or gently descending, it runs along the N ridge of Moosalamoo for about 0.8 mi and is moderately rough here. Then it swings around E, goes downhill and crosses two dirt roads in rapid succession after another mile. The trail then goes NW in a beautiful forest mostly of beech and through glades of ferns as pretty as you will find anywhere.

Follow a contour line, with little change in elevation, then climb a bit and descend by easy switchbacks through a stand of giant birches, coming out to a powerline. From here on the trail was not blazed in 1981, but the way is clear. Go L under the line, cross a substantial new bridge and descend on a jeep track that gradually becomes a dirt road. Stay on this road, descending finally to the paved road at Rt 125 (10.7 mi). Go L downhill to East Middlebury, alongside a handsome gorge which you cross on a stone bridge. The Wayberry Inn is 0.5 mi beyond the bridge. Rt 7 is 2.0 mi farther on.

SOUTH—Walk E from the Wayberry Inn in East Middlebury, on Rt 125, over a stone bridge and uphill. An unmarked dirt road going R (S) appears after 1.1 mi. Immediately after this a woods road enters just before a national forest sign (with a fire symbol). Go R on this woods road, and soon turn L in on an ascending dirt road. As you climb up this road keep L at any forks; follow the powerline cut until it goes L and cross a bridge. Beyond is a blue-blazed trail R (S). Follow the blazed trail up the N ridge of Mt Moosalamoo until it joins the Mt Moosalamoo Trail. Go L downhill to the Moosalamoo Campground and L out the access road to a gravel road. Go R (S) 2.2 mi to Blueberry Hill Inn.

skunk cabbage

GREYLOCK WALK
Massachusetts, 3 day circuit 26.9 miles (43.4 km)

SECTION	DISTANCE	OVERNIGHT POINTS
1	8.7 mi (14.0 km)	Williamstown-Mt Greylock
2	8.1 mi (13.1 km)	Mt Greylock-Cold Spring Road
3	10.1 mi (16.3 km)	Cold Spring Road-Williamstown

MAP—

W.O.C. Map of the Williamstown Area. Order from the Williams Outing Club, Williamstown, MA 01267.

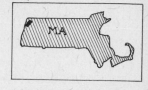

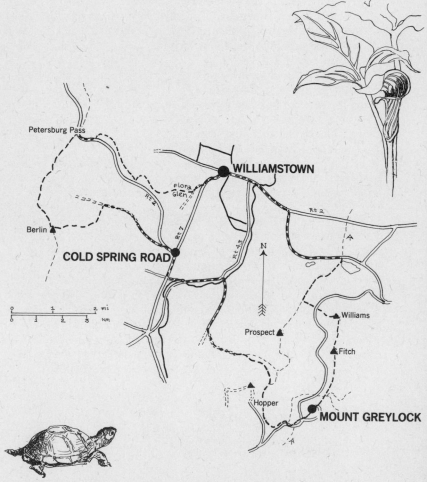

Petersburg Pass

WILLIAMSTOWN

Flora Glen

Rt 2

Berlin

Rt 7

COLD SPRING ROAD

Rt 43

N

Williams

Prospect

Fitch

Hopper

MOUNT GREYLOCK

Key: ● place, ▲ mountain, --- trail

64

TRANSPORTATION
Williamstown—bus (Vermont Transit) Pittsfield & New York
2 r/t dly
(Englander Coach) Boston 5 r/t dly

ACCOMMODATIONS (area code 413)

The Williams Inn	458-9371
Northside Inn	458-8107
Chimney Mirror Motel	458-5205
Four Acres Motel	458-8158
1896 House, Cold Spring Rd	458-8125
Ewal Pines, Cold Spring Rd	458-8161

Mt Greylock, Lanesboro, MA 01237

Bascom Lodge, PO Box 394	743-1591

This is a varied and fairly easy three-day circuit hike, starting and ending in Williamstown, in the little-populated northwest corner of Massachusetts. The centerpiece is Mt Greylock, the highest point in the state, where you spend the night at the recently renovated Bascom Lodge. The route climbs the long ridge of Mt Greylock from the north, on the Appalachian Trail, goes west down the odd-shaped Hopper Ravine to the valley of the Green River and continues west up to the top of the Taconic Range. You follow its ridgeline north on the Taconic Crest Trail from Berlin Mountain to Petersburg Pass and return down through woods and meadows to Williamstown. The contrast between wooded uplands and the open farmlands of the valley enhances the qualities of each. The trails are well maintained and marked by the Williams Outing Club, an energetic association of the college.

65

OVERNIGHT POINTS

Williamstown, once West Hoosuck, changed its name because a French and Indian War hero, Colonel Ephraim Williams, Jr, left a bequest in 1755 to establish a "free school" in the town if the town was renamed for him. The town fathers took 10 years to decide to accept. Over the years the school became the college it is today. Now Williamstown is a quiet college town, an unhurried place filled with students walking and bicycling. There is an art museum in the college's Lawrence Hall, and the Sterling and Francine Clark Art Institute, known for its collection of Winslow Homer paintings, is on South Street. Both are open year-round and are free. There is a Williamstown Summer Theater, late June through late August, a cinema and a few stores. The town has a number of handsome old houses set in wide lawns and is worth a stroll round in the evening. **Mount Greylock** (summit) hardly can be called developed, although it has two roads leading up to it. Bascom Lodge provides refreshments, meals and can take a limited number of overnight guests. Besides visiting the memorial tower beside the lodge and enjoying the society of the few other guests, hope for clear weather so you can feast on the view, which is worth the climb to this lofty perch. **Cold Spring Road** is simply several lodgings on the outskirts of Williamstown that make possible this circuit Walk.

1776 revisited

1. WILLIAMSTOWN—MOUNT GREYLOCK
8.7 mi (14.0 km) / 2890 ft (880 m)

This hike climbs from Williamstown to the top of Mt Greylock, where you have the rare pleasure of spending your night at the height of your hike instead of at the usual resting place below in the valley. The first part of the day is on a woodland path that climbs unremittingly up Mt Prospect. We hiked up on a clear sunny day in early May and all along the first part of the path we

66

marveled at the woodland beauty close at hand; surely a Japanese genius of a gardener had been here before us, adjusting the landscape to perfection, designing a series of small vignettes to lure us on. Masses of spring beauties, small clumps of trout lilies and individual wake-robins were each appropriately planted against the backgrounds that most effectively set them off—either a mossy rock, lichen-covered old stump or the ridged bark of a large tree trunk. The trail itself is ideally laid out, with small switchbacks fitting the contour of the mountain. We even had our hiking melody and rhythm set for us by the white-throated sparrow's song counterpoised against the miniature air-hammer staccato of a woodpecker. So bemused were we that it was only when we stopped at the top of the ridge for the look down to the town that we realized from our lack of breath and the pounding of our hearts what a steep climb it is.

The next part of the hike requires fewer pauses as it is through brush and a more uniform forest. It is challenging enough, with two summits to cross—Mt Williams (good view) and Mt Fitch (no view)—before you gain the top of Greylock with its spectacular views. If you are lucky you may even enjoy a sunset from there, one of the bonuses of spending the night on top. The footing is generally good and the way well marked.

SOUTH—Walk E on Main St (Rt 2) in Williamstown to Luce Hill Rd, 1.2 mi from the junctions of Rts 2 and 43. Go R (S) about 2.2 mi on this road. It swings E in 1.0 mi and passes Williamstown Reservoir. Just before a second reservoir (Mt Williams Reservoir), the Appalachian Trail (AT), blazed white, crosses the road. Go R through a stand of pines on the AT and on through a small grove of large birches whose thick white trunks are almost luminous against the surrounding greenery. Again go R downhill on a broad path, passing a dam, pool and several small camping areas. The trail begins to climb; you will catch glimpses of Mt Williams L and pass a blue-blazed trail. There is now some serious uphill hiking on a good trail leading to Mt Prospect's summit ridge, a rocky outcropping with splendid open views. Here (5.0 mi) the blue-blazed Mt Prospect Trail goes straight ahead, while the AT goes sharply L and descends through spruce to a clearing and a side trail marked "Wilbur Clearing Shelter via Muddy Brook Trail." Here the way becomes an old logging road which soon crosses a paved road (sign indicates "Mt Greylock via AT, 3.0 mi") and climbs to the top of Mt Williams (6.2 mi). At the summit there is a small rock outcrop with a good view and a register box.

From the summit you turn sharply S and descend in hairpin bends to the col between Mt William and Mt Fitch (6.6 mi). A side trail R leads to Notch Rd. From the col follow the crest of the long Greylock ridge, sometimes climbing or descending slightly, over Mt Fitch (no views) to Mt Greylock. At 8.2 mi cross a ski trail and join another. In 0.5 mi cross a paved road and ascend a short distance to the edge of the summit parking lot. The AT skirts the lot and soon reaches the summit memorial. Bascom Lodge is just beyond.

Bascom Lodge

NORTH—Pick up the white blazes of the AT at the summit memorial, and go N. Drop down past a parking lot and a road and join a ski trail for about 0.5 mi. Continue N as the ski trail swings E, and cross a second ski trail. The way down to Luce Hill Rd is well marked. The distances are Mts William/Fitch col 2.1 mi; Mt Williams 2.5 mi; junction Prospect Mt Trail 3.7 mi; Luce Hill Rd 5.2 mi. Go L on this road to Rt 2 (7.5 mi), and then L to Williamstown.

2. MT. GREYLOCK—COLD SPRING ROAD
8.1 mi (13.1 km)/2690 ft (820 m)
Half in wooded upland and half in lowland farms, this section shows the best of both worlds. It moves from the Greylock ridge to the Green River valley by the curiously shaped Hopper, whose square slanted sides look like a giant grain hopper (you see this best from the Taconic Crest Trail in Section 3). The farms are all being worked, and you may encounter cows at the woods edge as we did, intensely curious about two-legged intruders. City dwellers may be nervous about close bovine attention, but as long

as the cattle are the udder kind you have no worries; bulls are generally kept solitary.

We hiked this route in early May and were surprised to see two bow hunters in camouflage suits on the trail. They allowed as how they were turkey hunting. Turkey hunting! We thought wild turkeys had all but disappeared in the Northeast shortly after the Pilgrims invited them to the first Thanksgiving Dinner. The hunters said we might hear, as we hiked, the cocks gobbling to attract hens. And so it was; several times as we walked we heard the unmistakable gobble which we had only heard before from barnyard fowl. The hunters also told us that hunters made gobbling noises in order to attract the turkeys and regaled us with the hoary tale of the hunter who heard, as he gobbled away, another hunter nearby, also gobbling but doing a terrible job of it. Finally, feeling that the second hunter was driving any turkeys away, the first hunter started for home. Curiosity got the better of him, however, and he walked over to see the other hunter. There was a fine large turkey cock, gobbling away! We wondered if the Indians had started that story on its rounds.

WEST—From N end of Bascom Lodge go down the paved access road a short distance, past the TV building, to the white-blazed southbound AT going L. Follow it down through woods a short distance, cross a paved road back into the woods and come out on the paved road again. The AT crosses this road, but you go R to a blue-blazed woods road signposted "Williamstown 8 mi." Go R down this road 0.5 mi to paved road at a hairpin turn, and immediately go R again on another woods road. In about 0.2 mi the blue blazes lead you R by a brook (red-blazed Deer Hill Trail goes ahead) on a trail going down to a dirt road at the entrance to Sperry Campground.

Go R into the campground on the dirt road and R again into the woods, on a blue-blazed path (The Hopper Trail) which soon turns into a woods road running down the S side of the Hopper. At the bottom you cross a meadow beginning to be over grown with trees. The blazes here are found on the rocks; they end at a farm road and signpost, pointing to the Hopper Trail the way you have come and the Money Brook Trail to the R. Go L (W) out the tree-lined farm road (closing gates behind you) to Haley Farm (4.1 mi), and walk out the gravel farm access road to the paved Green River Rd (Rt 43) at Sweets Corner (6.2 mi). Go L 0.5 mi to Scotts Hill Rd and R to Cold Spring Rd (Rt 7, 7.5 mi). Go R on Cold Spring Rd to its junction with Rt 2. The 1896 House and Ewal Pines are 0.5 mi farther on Rt 7.

EAST—Walk 0.5 mi S on Cold Spring Rd (Rt 7) from its southern junction with Rt 2 to the first road L (Fox Hill Rd). Take Fox Hill Rd to Green River Rd (Rt 43), and go L along the river to Sweets Corner and gravel Hopper Rd (first public road R). Go R on Hopper Rd and L (W) at the first fork to Haley's Farm (4.0 mi). Continue W on a farm track, a continuation of the farm access road, to a signpost, and go R on blue-blazed Hopper Trail to Sperry Campground. Here go L on a dirt road to blue-blazed trail going L uphill, which meets the white-blazed AT at the top of the Greylock ridge. The summit of Mt Greylock and Bascom Lodge are on the AT 0.5 mi L.

wake robin

3. COLD SPRING ROAD—WILLIAMSTOWN
10.1 mi (16.3 km) / 1980 ft (600 m)
This section gives you a taste of the Taconic Crest Trail, which follows the top of the Taconic Range 29 miles south from the Vermont border. The range forms the boundary between Massachusetts and New York, and you may be walking with a foot in each state. The hike includes Berlin Mountain, the highest of the Taconic summits. You climb to the crest from the Green River

70

Valley through woods, follow the ridge for a distance and then descend through woods and meadows to Williamstown. There are excellent views at a number of points along the Crest Trail and from the high meadows near Petersburg Pass.

We were chaperoned over this section by a very large but friendly black German shepherd dog. His collar announced that he was Bear, and so he answered. He frolicked happily around us and refused to be sent back. So there were three of us that day. He growled at every other hiker until near them, and then he licked their hands (to their considerable relief). He waited patiently for us if we lagged and at lunch begged food only in a gentlemanly manner. Great company indeed! At day's end, since he showed no signs of wanting to go home, we called the number on his collar. It was for a veterinarian 40 miles away and the vet wasn't home. So, after a heated family discussion about what to do with Bear, we reluctantly walked him to the Police Station. The officers on duty were so cordial to us and Bear greeted them so like long-lost friends (they had never seen him before) that our reluctance vanished and we left, secure in the knowledge that they would treat each other well.

NORTH—From the junctions of Rts 2 and 7, 2.5 mi S of Williamstown, walk W on Rt 2 to Torrey Woods Rd and take the latter L 1.5 mi to a blue-blazed trail L. This takes you through the woods for 0.5 mi to a campsite by a brook. Cross the brook to a woods road running above the S bank, and go W uphill. After a short distance you leave the woods road and climb steeply to the top of the E spur of Berlin Mt. Red and yellow blazes come in from the L and join the blue blazes. There is a stand of hemlocks here and good views E.

Continue climbing on a more gradual grade until you reach a grassy road. Go L to the open summit of Berlin Mt (2798 ft) 3.4 mi from Cold Spring Rd. After enjoying the panoramic views,

hairy woodpecker

71

especially E of Mt Greylock and the square-sided Hopper and S of the long ridge of the Taconic Trail, walk N down the summit access road (white diamond markers at short intervals). This road leads along the ridge through open woods down to Berlin Pass, crossed by the remains of the old Albany Post Rd, now the Berlin Pass Trail to the E (not marked). To the R downhill is the cleared area of a ski slope and ahead the ridge is covered by a heath. Go up the heath into woods still following white diamonds, continue N along the W side of the ridge for 0.5 mi and climb R a short distance to the top of the Petersburg Pass ski slopes. Follow the W edge of the novice slope (the most westerly slope) down to the parking lot and Rt 2 (6.1 mi). Before going E (R) down Rt 2 for 0.5 mi, look down and locate a cut of an old powerline through the trees off its L side. This is where you leave Rt 2 and it is easy to miss from the road.

After several bends in Rt 2 you pass back into Massachusetts (so marked) and should start looking for your trailhead. When you come to a pair of ''no passing'' signs on opposite sides of the road, the L one rectangular and the R one a yellow triangular flag, look carefully L. A small tree on top of the steep side of the road has a blue blaze, and by scrambling up the scree you will reach the old powerline route. Follow it up and then downhill until it turns R (a red blaze with a blue center here as well as a double blue blaze) on an old woods road. In a bit a red-blazed trail comes in R, which you ignore. Continue ahead, now paralleling Rt 2 which you occasionally glimpse and hear on your R. The woods road ends at a dirt road coming off Rt 2. Go L, passing a parking place with a sign ''Taconic Trails State Park.'' There is a lovely open field R with a view down to Williamstown and across to Mt Greylock.

Greylock

Continue on the dirt road until you see a double line of trees going R, separating one meadow from the next. Go R along this line of trees on an old farm road, and pick up blue blazes. The road soon ends in the meadow. Ahead somewhat to the R is an old foundation. Pass it (you will find a blue blaze on its far R corner) and head E downhill through the field to its SE corner where you will enter the woods on a blue-blazed path. This path continues E through a wet section with many log bridges. In 0.8 mi you enter a stand of pines and come alongside a good-sized stream at the head of Flora Glen. The easy path clings to the side of the glen above a stream, then heads down to a pool and dam where you meet the unpaved Bee Hill Rd. Go L down to Rt 7. Williamstown is 0.8 mi L.

SOUTH—Walk S on Rt 7 from Williamstown 0.8 mi to Bee Hill Rd. Go R up Bee Hill Rd until you see a sign, "R.R.R. Brook," on the R. As you step off the road you'll see a small dam. Go to its S end and pick up a trail going up Flora Glen (blue blazes). When you reach a long narrow field, go uphill until it widens out; head for an old foundation and then to a double line of trees ending at a dirt road. Go L, and when almost at a paved road (Rt 2), take a trail R uphill; follow the blue blazes. This carries you to an old powerline (now poleless) that leads to Rt 2.

Go R uphill to Petersburg Pass, L into the ski area parking lot. Go up W side of the W novice slope, and pick up white diamond blazes to a trail R leading down to a woods road running S along W side of the ridge. This carries you down to Berlin Pass and up to the summit of Berlin Mt (6.7 mi). At the summit go E (L) down a grassy road to a blue-and-red blazed trail, and follow the blue blazes down to a gravel road (8.9 mi). Go R to Rt 2 and R down Rt 2 to its junction with Rt 7. The lodgings are 0.5 mi L on Rt 7.

73

CAPE COD WALK
Massachusetts, 4 days, 32.4 miles (52.3 km)

MAP—
Millers Map of Provincetown
Truro, Wellfleet, Eastham.
Order from The Butterworth
Co., 23 Trader Lane, West Y
mouth, MA 02673
(617-775-4438 for price).

SECTION	DISTANCE		OVERNIGHT POINTS
1	12.2 mi	(19.7 km)	Eastham-Wellfleet
2	8.1 mi	(13.1 km)	Wellfleet-Truro
3	8.1 mi	(13.1 km)	Truro-Pilgrim Lake
4	4.0 mi	(6.5 km)	Pilgrim Lake-Provincetown East End
4a	9.5 mi	(15.3 km)	Pilgrim Lake-Provincetown via Cape Race

74

TRANSPORTATION
All Points—bus (Cape Code Bus lines), Hyannis, bus
        Boston/NYC 2 r/t dly

Provincetown—boat (**Provincetown**) Boston 1 r/t dly
        —air (Provincetown-Boston Airline)
        —Boston 3 r/t dly

ACCOMMODATIONS (area code 617)
Eastham, MA 02642
        Salt Pond Inn, Box 397   255-2100
        Eastham Motel, Box 428   255-1600

Wellfleet, MA 02667
        Inne at Ducke Creeke, PO Box 364   394-9333
        Holden Inn, PO Box 816   349-3450
        The Moorings, PO Box 704   349-3379

Truro, MA 02666
        Whitman House   487-1740
        Gingerbread House   349-2596
        Shady Rest Cottages, PO Box 172   349-9410

North Truro, MA 02652
        Truro Motor Inn, PO Box 364   487-3628

Pilgrim Lake, North Truro, MA 02652
        Outer Reach Resort Motel   487-0629
        Cape Breeze Motel   487-9110

Provincetown MA 02657
        P-town East End—Sand Castle Waterfront Resort 487-9300
                Holiday Shores Motel   487-9175

        P-town proper—write or call Provincetown Chamber of
                Commerce, PO Box 1017,   487-3424.

For eastern hikers conditioned to the idea that good hikes are only in deep woods along mountain ridges and summits, this Walk will be a complete and pleasant surprise. It is one of a kind, combining comfortable places to stay with unspoiled beaches, sand heaths, dunes and quiet coastal woodlands. Anyone used to humanity-packed beaches will find it doubly astounding to come upon this long stretch of uninterrupted natural land jutting out into the sea. We can thank the many people who fought for the Cape Cod National Seashore, through which most of this Walk goes, for preserving this area from commercial and residential development and for protecting its fragile ecosystem.

The land over which you hike, oddly called the Lower Cape, is the remains of a vast glacial terminal moraine. Here 10,000 years ago the forward edge of the ice sheet dropped its load of sand, gravel and stones which it had scraped from mountains during its journey from the north. Since then, wind and tide have worked together to redistribute this glacial till while vegetation has sought to stabilize it. It has been an unequal struggle, which erosion is winning. At the end of the last ice age, Cape Cod stopped at the Highlands of North Truro. The ocean has since stolen from the Atlantic side of this great moraine and redeposited the sand elsewhere, principally in the curving claw of the Province Lands and Provincetown. By the time the Mayflower appeared, this work had largely been completed and the Lower Cape was covered by a dense forest; beach erosion had been slowed but not stopped.

The coming of the colonists changed this relatively stable situation in only a few short years. By 1630 Plymouth, the original settlement of the Pilgrims (who arrived in 1620), was growing crowded, and people were beginning to move to the Cape. Eastham, on the Lower Cape, was settled first in 1644, and colonists moved slowly north until, by the end of the century, farms were scattered all along the Cape. The forests began to disappear, first to furnish farmland, building material and firewood, then to support the industries that followed; they provided wood for ships' ribs and planks, wood for burning to extract potash, wood for boiling seawater for its salt and wood to make charcoal for the bog iron furnaces. By 1700 inland dunes appeared and began their march as the thin topsoil was no longer held by the forests. Alarmed settlers early passed ordinances to save the remaining woods and planted beach grass to check the dunes. The damage these few early decades wrought has since been under repair, by happenstance and design, for nearly 300 years, and much of the Lower Cape is now reforested. But there are still heaths, where only low-growing plants hold the soil, and the moving dunes still claim five miles of the land north of the Truro Highlands.

We have dwelled on this history because it will help explain the land through which you will hike. You will pass miles of Atlantic beach cliff, still being eroded by the sea (some three feet per year) in spite of what nature and man can do. You will walk through woods and meadows and return to woods, finding not the large trees found by the settlers but respectable forests nonetheless. You will see the heaths and miles of land covered with dune grass where land reclamation commences (please stay on the path so that you don't join the colonists and make a new desert). And lastly, you will visit the great dunes, still marching on the green land, deadly in their slow effect but with a stark, compelling beauty.

While your days are spent hiking over this varied terrain, your overnight points reflect more recent history. As the soil was too thin to support farming for very long, the people soon turned to fishing and whaling for a living, and until tourism came, this was the principal industry. You will visit and stay in the charming seaport of Wellfleet, filled with well-kept houses of the 1880s and a dozen or so unobtrusive art galleries, and the quite different seaport of Truro, whose houses are scattered as if the original builders wanted a deal of elbow room. The Walk starts at the Salt Pond Visitor Center in Eastham, once a seaport but now a tourist area. Salt Pond is a perfect place to begin to see what Cape Cod National Seashore has to offer. From here you work your way north to Provincetown—partly by beach along the ever-changing Atlantic Ocean, past lighthouses and the site where Marconi sent the first transatlantic radio message; partly by shady woods and ponds; and partly through the Province Lands desert.

You will inevitably be drawn to recognize and appreciate the progression of plant life this living laboratory presents, as you move inland from the harsh environment at the sea's edge to the salt meadows, swamps and woods. Here you will find kettle ponds, freshwater lakes filling the depressions made by blocks of glacial ice. The National Seashore Centers have displays, movies and pamphlets to help you to orient yourself to this intriguing land. We found that reading and studying our own reference books before the trip was a help in identifying what we encountered. The most common flora near the beach are beach plum, dusty miller, beach heather and beach rose. Bear oak, bayberry and stunted pitch pines soon follow. Farther inland these pines increase in size and are joined by beeches and maples and, in some instances, Atlantic white cedar. Since we share this generation's guilt for efficiently despoiling the environment, it is nice to know that in this case, we of the 19th and 20th centuries have been repairing the damage done by our forefathers of the 17th and 18th centuries. This land someday will once again be what the first settlers found.

If you have time before you go, read at least one of the two Cape Cod classics, Henry David Thoreau's *Cape Cod* and Henry Beston's *The Outermost House*. The two authors are separated by 75 years but united in their sensitive observation of the Cape's natural charms and in their ability to communicate vividly what they experienced.

Cape Cod is heavily crowded in July and August and somewhat crowded on good weekends in late May and June. Some places are closed October to May, so check out your overnight stops well in advance and, of course, always make reservations before you leave home.

OVERNIGHT POINTS

Eastham is reputedly where a landing party from the Mayflower, searching for a place to settle, encountered their first Indians, and the event took place, naturally, at First Encounter Beach at the foot of Samoset Road. The town was the first one settled on the northern arm of the Cape; seven men and their families moved here from Plymouth in 1644. One, Thomas Prence, served as governor of Massachusetts Bay Colony for 19 years. The town's history is the usual one for the Cape—farming, fishing and finally farming again as the fishing industry died. The old wind-driven Eastham Grist Mill, built in 1688 in Plymouth and moved to Eastham in 1793, is in working order and open to the public in the summer (May-Oct, 10-5 Mon-Sat, 1-5 Sun). It is on the village green, Rt 6 and Samoset Road, south of the Salt Pond Visitor Center. Farther south 0.8 mi is the self-guided Fort Hill Nature Trail which circles through old farmland and along Nauset Marsh. **Wellfleet** was originally called Billingsgate (from an area in London noted for its fishmongers). The town was an active seaport, with fishing, oystering, whaling and trading the principal occupations. The railroad and steamships ended this prosperity in the 1880s. Architecturally, time stood still the next 100 years. The town center is a homogeneous collection of well-kept houses from the 19th century. By no means a museum piece, the town is alive with year-round residents, and tourists are only a modest and unobtrusive addition. You will want to stroll around town—along Main Street with its small cluster of shops; along Commercial Street which parallels Duck Creek, where deep-sea vessels once tied up, but which is now a quiet silted backwater; and down to the harbor, alive with fishing boats and pleasure craft. You can take a sunset trip on the bay from the town pier (Tues and Thurs evenings, mid-May to Columbus Day). The town clock, on the steeple of the First Congregational Church, is claimed to be the only town clock which strikes ship's time (striking one to eight bells on the half-hour over each four-hour period, corresponding to the length of a ship's company watch or duty). Wellfleet is noted for its art galleries, of which a dozen are scattered through the town. There is a small museum on Main Street (open late June–mid-Sept, Tues-Sat, 2-5 pm) and the Samuel Rider House on Gull Pond Road which has an exhibit of the Wellfleet Historical Society's collection of the town's history (open late June-Labor Day, Mon-Fri, 2-5 pm). The Audubon Society has a well-known wildlife sanctuary on the bay between Eastham and Wellfleet. It does not lie very near our route so, alas, would have

to be visited another time. Truro is the least densely populated of
the Cape towns, and it is hard to find. There is no visible town
center, in the form of a close cluster of houses and shops; the
houses are scattered among the fields and woods in the loose farming pattern of the early settlers. The harbor at the foot of Depot
Street, once busy with a forest of fishing boat masts, now has only
a few craft. It is difficult for tired hikers to explore this scattered
area. **Pilgrim Lake** is not a settlement at all, but the beginning of
the concentrated tourist development of Provincetown motels,
guest houses and cottages which stretches west for four miles. It is
at the end of the Truro Highlands, once the end of the Cape. You
will be staying either on the edge of this highland or along the
narrow sand causeway which changed Pilgrim Lake from a bay into a brackish pond. **Provincetown East End** is at the other end of
the sand causeway which closes off Pilgrim Lake. It takes two
rather dull miles through a line of tourist accommodations to
reach the center of Provincetown, too far to walk of an evening.
Provincetown is an example of how a once quiet fishing town, little frequented by outsiders, can be changed by tourist occupation
into a busy, crowded mixture of old quaintness and new commer-
cialism. The miracle is that despite all this new intrusion its
charms are still there if one takes the time and effort to seek them.
NOTE ON BEACHWALKING—We recommend that you time
your beach hiking to be near low tide, and preferably while the
tide is still ebbing. You will find the sand to be its firmest, the
beach its widest, and there will be more to see. Avoid high tide if
possible, especially during spring tides—periods when the sun
and moon produce maximum tidal heights—as the sea will cover
the beaches right up to the cliffs in places and leave you no room
to pass. Heavy northeasters will have strong onshore winds causing
the walking to be strenuous and even unpleasant. In any event,
try the beach. If you find it more pain than pleasure, there are
"escape" points every mile or two; we describe ways to minimize
beachwalking below.

We found the sand on the beach here to be relatively soft
underfoot even at the best of tidal conditions. We are used to the
very hard sand left by a receding tide on the Jersey shore where
one can even ride a bike. Not so here. One has to hunt constantly
for the firmest sand relative to the surf line, and you should expect
a slower pace and more exertion than its level smoothness sug-
gests.

We recommend that honest-to-goodness ocean swimming be
done at the guarded public beaches through which you will pass.

However, at low tide there are many quiet pools protected by sandbars where paddling is perfectly safe. But be warned: the water stays co-old all year. Bayside or inland pond waters are much more temperate.

There may be times when you want to avoid hiking on the beach because of unusually high tides or winds. The map we recommend shows all the back roads, so you can work out off-beach routes yourself. However, there is an interesting off-beach hike between Marconi Beach and LeConte Hollow Road that the map does not show. If you go off the Beach at Marconi Beach, take the Marconi Beach Road to the Marconi Site Road, and walk to the Marconi Site (be sure to visit the interpretive shelter describing the Marconi Wireless Station). Take the self-guided Atlantic White Cedar Swamp Trail, which leaves from the south end of the parking lot. You will do the first and most interesting leg of this trail (pick up a pamphlet at the start). At the end of the boardwalk through the swamp, go L (E) on a dirt road to the first crossroad, also dirt. This latter is the Old Wireless Road which once served the Wireless Site. The nature trail goes R from this junction back to the parking lot, but you go L (N) on the Old Wireless Road. In 10 minutes you will pass a barrier (boundary of the National Seashore) and in another 5 minutes come out on the LeConte Hollow Road. Go R to Ocean View Road or on back to the beach.

WHAT TO BRING—An adjustment is necessary to our regular advice on what to bring (see p 186). Leave your hiking boots home. Comfortable sneakers or light walking shoes are better since the hiking boots seem to sink deeper into the sand than lighter footwear. You may even find yourself taking to bare feet on the beach. Tuck in a bathing suit or other airy garment because you may get a midsummer day even in spring or late autumn. Don't leave your warm sweater and raingear at home however, for even in midsummer you may also get the other extremes of cold wind and/or cold rain. The weather, like the terrain, tends to quick changes.

TRAIL DATA—On this Walk we deviate from our usual procedure of giving trail data for both directions of travel (except for Section 4). The map we recommend is clear, and we feel you will have no difficulty in reversing our description and charting your own way.

There are no signposts anywhere on the beach; therefore, in order to know when to exit, you will have to keep track of the easily identifiable points by recognizing them for what they are—lighthouse, public beach). We have listed these landmarks with their mileage north and south, for your reference. All the points are public, except as noted.

Distance, in miles, of Lower Cape Beach "Mileposts"

		N	S
Eastham	Coast Guard Beach	0	24.9
	Nauset Light Beach	1.8	23.1
Wellfleet	Marconi Beach	3.2	21.7
	Marconi Site*	5.1	19.8
	Lecount Hollow Beach	5.9	19.0
	White Crest Beach	6.4	18.5
	Cahoon Hollow Beach	7.6	17.3
	Newcomb Hollow Beach	9.1	15.8
Truro	Pamet (Ballston) Beach	12.0	12.9
	Long Nook Beach	13.7	11.2
	Cape Cod Light**	15.3	9.6
	Highland Beach	16.4	8.5
	Head of the Meadow Beach	16.9	8.0
	High Head	18.9	6.0
	Access to Great Dunes	20.9	4.0
Provincetown	Race Point Beach	24.9	0

*no public exit from beach
**emergency exit only, see Section 3

beach plum

1. EASTHAM—WELLFLEET

12.2 mi (19.7 km)

This section is a perfect introduction to Cape Cod hiking since you experience both the ocean beach and the wooded interior. It is the longest hike of the four days, but has a rewarding ending at Wellfleet, the most charming village on the Lower Cape. You start in Eastham at the Salt Pond Visitor Center of the Cape Cod National Seashore, walk through woods and meadows to the beach, stroll for miles along the constantly changing shoreline and come finally by quiet back roads to Wellfleet. Before you start, visit the Visitor Center to see the exhibits and short film (9-5 daily).

Beach walking is unlike any other perambulation. For many of us it is tied to childhood memories—building sandcastles, surf bathing, sun bathing and collecting shells and beach flotsam and jetsam. You can indulge in all these activities, at the penalty of slowing your progress and burdening your knapsack, or you may simply watch the unfolding scenery. The cliff and dune surfaces are never the same from one point or from one day to another. The surf line changes with the tide with low tide revealing pools of fish and shells. The shell population is low except after storms, but in its stead are stretches of beach pebbles of a variety of shapes and colors, ranging from translucent white beach "diamonds" to single-toned stones to speckled pebbles looking like eggs. As for bird life, there will always be the common herring gull somewhere about. The Atlantic side of the Cape seemed to have only a few birds when we were there (late May), and we missed the little wading birds that scurry along the beach at the surf line—sandpipers and killdeer. But keep an eye on the beach, aloft and out to sea to catch glimpses of gulls, terns and ducks. On the few cliffs of clay, you will see swallows darting in and out of their nesting holes in the steep face.

NORTH—Leave the Salt Pond Visitor Center, just off Rt 6 in Eastham, on the bicycle trail which starts at the parking lot. An early but worthwhile digression is to leave by the self-guided Nauset Marsh Trail which starts at the amphitheater behind the Center. It adds perhaps 0.3 mi to your day's walk. Pick up a folder at the Center before you take the trail. It intersects the bike trail, and you go R on this bicycle path by oak-pine woods and through fields dotted with Eastern red cedar (juniper) to the Coast Guard station and beach (1.6 mi).

If you did not elect to go via the Nauset Marsh Trail, there is a short and interesting digression from the bike trail that shows you Nauset Bay. When the trail crosses a road marked "Doane Rock" to the L and "Doane Memorial" to the R, go R to a clearing where the site of Deacon John Doane's homestead is marked. Doane, one of the seven original settlers of Nauset, later Eastham, came to this area in 1644. A path leads from here down to and along the shore of Nauset Bay and rejoins the bicycle trail shortly before it crosses a marsh on a long wooden footbridge. This side path provides a close-up view of the bay edge and is a nice change from the bike trail.

At the end of the bridge take a short path of crushed oyster shells R to the old Coast Guard station. There is a tablet here about the Mayflower's first encounter with the New World with a tracing of her route. Beyond the station you get your first evidence of the sea's work on the land—a 1978 storm took away the old parking lot and much of the headland here. Descend to the beach

Nauset Light

and start your beach trek N (L). It is a beautiful stretch of beach, and if you get one of those frequent jewel-like days, we defy you to walk along it without a feeling of exhilaration. The lighthouse (Nauset Light) appearing on the skyline after a mile is pure New England post card—a squat red tower with a large reflector light. Close by to the L is a smaller, dirty white-shingled lighthouse. Why two so close together? We learned later that the second is a retired lighthouse moved to the site for a private residence. Beyond the lighthouse you have another 6.5 mi of beach with growing and shrinking cliffs and an irregular water's edge. The public beaches tend to be at points where the cliffs are low, for easy access, but not always. Each access point appears as a break in the cliff, well trampled by feet, or as a set of wooden stairs. Most of the points are not very distinctive, so keep track of them as you pass. In succession you will pass from Coast Guard Beach, Nauset Light Beach N of the lighthouse, Marconi Beach, Marconi Site, visible only as a fence along the cliff edge and a glimpse of the interpretive shelter, Lecount Hollow Beach and White Crest Beach. At 7.6 mi from Coast Guard Beach and 9.2 mi from Salt Pond Visitor Center, you will reach Cahoon Hollow Beach and leave the ocean here. You can recognize this beach access point as you climb to the parking lot because, in the little hollow just back of the beach, there is an old Life Saving station, now open as a disco in the summer. It was one of 13 that protected the Lower Cape, the first was built in 1879 and the others were added soon afterwards. From each station men patrolled the beach on each side, meeting men from the adjoining stations at halfway huts. They watched for vessels in distress and if necessary ran back for help to the stations for lifeboats. The halfway houses were kept stocked with food and firewood in case mariners came ashore in bitter weather. Thoreau writes of these "charity" huts in *Cape Cod*.

Go out the beach access road a short distance to Ocean View Drive, turn R and walk to Long Pond Rd. This is a quiet paved road that goes L through woods past some secluded homes down into Wellfleet 3.0 mi from Cahoon. About 1.0 mi from Ocean View Dr the road skirts Long Pond where you will pass a small public picnic area and swimming beach. The water here should be much warmer than the chilly Atlantic if you wish to use your bathing suit. Shortly before Wellfleet the road passes over Rt 6 and reaches Main St. The Inne at Ducke Creek is L. Jog R to E Commercial St for the other listed lodgings.

2. WELLFLEET—TRURO
8.1 mi (13.1 km)
This is similar to the Eastham-Wellfleet section, a walk by quiet country roads to and from the beach and a hike along the shore. You will see few people since there is a three-mile stretch of beach without any public access. There are two routes available off the beach into Truro, depending on where you spend the night.

What is poor weather for vacationers may be ideal for the hiker so long as your raingear is handy. The day we walked this section was an unsettled one. This gave us the whole beach to ourselves—a wonderful feeling! Such days are more interesting than bright sunny ones, because of the changing aspects of land, sea and sky and the excitement of not knowing just what the weather will be like ahead. Broken clouds were scudding across the sky and casting moving shadows along the beach. Ahead it would be black and foreboding, or the sun would pick out a curve of golden sand and turquoise water—a luminous promise shining out of the surrounding gloom. Alternately, there were times when

Wellfleet clock

the view behind was a beautiful but frightening black, while ahead there was pale grey mist blotting out beach and sea; while over us the sky was a serene blue. It was a day of constant change from one minute to the next. Luckily for us a hard shower waited until we were off the beach and under the shelter of some trees.

You will feel as if you are walking straight along the water's edge and the rapidity with which the landmarks behind disappear from view will surprise you, evidence, of course, of the curve you are actually following.

NORTH—Walk N on School Rd, which runs off Main St E of the post office to Mill Hill Rd, and cross Rt 6 to Gross Hill Rd. Gull Pond Rd comes in from the L 1.2 mi from Rt 6. Gross Hill Rd now skirts Gull Pond but only close enough for the water to be glimpsed through the trees. In another 0.8 mi you reach Ocean View Rd. Go L to the Newcomb Hollow Rd and then R down to Newcomb Hollow Beach, 2.7 mi from Wellfleet.

The cliffs are high along this section of beach and the beach itself is not overly wide, so that high tide would force you much too close for comfort to these walls of sand that look susceptible to landslides. We noticed, in fact, several small slides in progress on the cliff face, with sand pouring down in miniature cascades. Notice the variety of surfaces the wind and water have sculptured into the face of the cliff—rounded, concave or rippled. Infrequently, there are places their searching fingers have missed, where oases of dusty miller, beach grass or beach heather cling tenaciously. You soon come to a sag in the cliffs giving way to an open area, a unique sight along the Lower Cape beach. There is a path into it, with the sign ''closed to motor vehicles.'' The hillside behind, stepped back from the beach, forms the rim of a half-bowl, and narrow paths in the green ground cover invite you to climb the bowl's sides. How like a Scottish moor scene it is! Remember how far you still have to go (about 4.0 mi), and judge your strength and time accordingly before accepting the invitation.

The beach cliffs rise again for a short way but soon become lower. Ahead you will see a steep headland with three buildings silhouetted against the sky. This is your landmark for Pamet Beach. If you are staying at Gingerbread House, you will leave the beach here (5.6 mi). There is a sandy right-of-way between snow fences that takes you to S Pamet Rd, which ends in a small parking lot. Go L on the road and climb to a high ridge giving views over the marshy Pamet River. You will pass a farm on the L and skirt the salt marshes.

At 1.0 mi pass Collins Rd, and at 1.7 mi go under Rt 6, ending quickly at Castle Rd. Here is all there is to the center of Truro—a post office, laundry and small restaurant. Jog L to Depot Rd and go R on it, past another salt marsh. At a small monument the road forks, with Old Country Rd going L. Go R on Depot Rd and you will soon see Gingerbread House, 2.5 mi from Pamet Beach. A nice walk after dinner leads down Depot Rd to the town landing on the bay, a delightful half-mile along marshes to tidal Truro Harbor.

If your lodgings are along Rt 6 N of Truro, you should continue past Pamet Beach another 1.7 mi to Long Nook Beach, the next public access. In May 1981 the sea had removed easy egress. You will follow a slanting path up a sloping sand cliff, worn by many feet, to a small parking lot at Long Nook Rd. Walk W on this road for 1.8 mi to Rt 6, through a hollow with high wooded land on each side, including a small beech forest. There are a few small farms, and the feeling is entirely rural. Go R (N) on Rt 6 for 0.5 mi for the Whitman House and Truro Motor Inn and L 0.5 mi for the Shady Rest Cottages.

horseshoe crab

3. TRURO—PILGRIM LAKE
8.1 mi (13.1 km)

The southern end of this hike is the now-usual walk through woodland and small farms and a hike along the beach. What is different is the stroll along a bicycle path that was once the Kings Highway, through the Meadows where salt hay was grown by early settlers. The northern end of the Walk is at what was originally the north edge of Cape Cod, the glacially deposited Truro Highlands. Behind you lie the woods that have now re-covered most of Cape Cod, ahead is the largely treeless dune country and brackish Pilgrim Lake.

The cliffs in this section, the highest on the Cape, reach 175 feet at Cape Cod Light, whose site was selected partly for that reason. The composition of the cliffs varies from all-sand steep slopes to clay vertical bluffs, although the latter are infrequent. In a few places vegetation has succeeded in covering the slopes. In other places there are dark horizontal lines in the cliff face, remains of land surfaces which were in place long enough to have vegetation form a thin layer of topsoil but which were subsequently covered by shifting sand. We counted as many as five of these old layers; one layer may be as much as 50 feet above another, which is a lot of drifted sand. We wondered why the sand would drift, stop long enough for soil to be formed and then drift again, all long before the colonists began their tampering with nature. Perhaps the cause was fires set by Indians or lightning. We noticed blocks of peat lying on the beach, indicating that swampy areas existed long enough for a substantial layer of dead vegetable matter to form. This can also be seen in a few places on the cliff face. We learned that in Eastham, when the forests were all cleared and none were left even for firewood, an Irish immigrant showed the settlers how to cut, dry and burn the peat.

89

Cape Cod Light

NORTH—From the Gingerbread House, walk R (E) on Depot Rd, jog L on Castle Rd to Pamet Rd and go R on Pamet. Just after the underpass under Rt 6, go L on N Pamet Rd, winding up and down hills of unspoiled woods and heath. It is less inhabited than S Pamet Rd, with dirt paths going N into wild areas that look worth a day's ramble. In about 1.5 mi you reach the end of the road at a driveway up to three buildings on a headland. A path goes S under this headland, skirting a marsh on your R, to the end of S Pamet Rd and the beach access point. Pamet was once a circular road but drifting sand cut it into two separate segments. Although the two roads start and end at the same points, walking each gives surprisingly different aspects of the countryside, one more example of that wonderful variety that is packed into the small area of the Lower Cape. From Pamet Beach go N 1.7 mi to Long Nook Beach. If you have stayed on Rt 6 near Castle Rd, you will reverse the directions from Section 2 and go S to Long Nook Rd and out to the beach. Go N from Long Nook Beach and enjoy the changing cliffs, the beach and water. The first visible landmark is Cape Cod Light (first built in 1797, with the present structure built in 1857). It is one of the few lighthouses in the U.S. still manned—most are now automatic. You first see an antenna, then a flagpole and finally the lighthouse itself, 1.6 mi from Long Nook. S of the light a sag in the cliff, with evidence of many feet scrambling up and down leads to the edge of the Highlands golf course. This is not a public access point but can be used as an emergency escape point, if needed. Beyond the light the cliff becomes a near-vertical clay face pocked with the holes made by nesting swallows. In season, they will be swooping in and out of the holes by regiments.

Farther N you will pass private wooden stairs going up to Hiland Cottages and 1.1 mi from the light pass Highland Beach. The cliffs begin to diminish in height and you soon reach the low openings giving access to Head of the Meadow Beach. At very low tide you may see just N of here the remains of the German bark

Francis that came ashore in 1873. Go past the first access point to Head of the Meadow Beach (wide and heavily used, beyond which a parking lot is visible), to a second smaller exit leading to a second parking lot not visible from the beach (there are two other small exits leading to this parking lot). At the SE corner of this lot pick up the bicycle trailhead. The trail goes along a salt meadow that runs between the dunes along the ocean and the edge of the Truro Highlands. A salt marsh once formed in this protected area. The colonists made dikes to dry out these marshes and turned them into salt meadows on which they grazed cattle and sheep and from which they cut salt hay. Hence the name of the public beach.

You are on the original land route to Provincetown, called the King's Highway. On your map you will see segments of this highway all along the Lower Cape. It was a path long trodden but, oddly, did not get its present name until after the U.S. had secured its independence. In late May there were carpets of spring wild flowers on each side of the narrow path. A profusion of cinnamon ferns, with their erect plumes like large green feathers, also lined the way—refreshing after the austere sand and water of the beach. Shrubbery partly hides the meadow most of the way, but there are occasional open places or short paths where you can step aside and get a good view of it. Your eyes and ears will tell you that the birds enjoy it even more than you do, and avid bird watchers better allow extra time for this bit. About a mile along the way there is a cleared picnic site identified as Pilgrim Spring, where a small group of Pilgrims under John Smith, exploring Cape Cod for the first time, recorded that they refreshed themselves. We commemorated this by a swig from our canteens.

Continuing on, you will soon come to another picnic table on the R that gives the best view of the meadow. From here, the vegetation becomes lower and less varied and the trail is much more out in the open. You will pass an old dike and soon reach a parking lot 2.0 mi from Head of the Meadow Beach. Go L 0.6 mi on a paved road to Rt 6. Lodgings are to the L on Rt 6 or 6a.

4. PILGRIM LAKE—PROVINCETOWN EAST END OR VIA CAPE RACE

4.0 mi (6.5 km) or 9.5 mi (15.3 km)

We include here hikes of different lengths and routes to fit your time and interests. We suggest, if you have half a day, that you walk the beach for two miles north of High Head and then cut inland and savor the remarkable dunes that stretch north for miles, ending at Provincetown East End. This combines a bit of beach walking and a smattering of the dunes. If you can take a little more time you can see more of the dunes by slogging along an interior dune buggy track from High Head. The distance is not much greater, but the walking is slow as you move from the tops of dunes down into deep basins; once meadows, these areas were changed by overgrazing into near-deserts. If you have a full day you can walk the beach to Provincetown via Cape Race.

BEACH WALK, WEST—Leave Rt 6 and go N on unmarked High Head Rd, which runs off Rt 6 at the S end of Pilgrim Lake, very near a short connecting road between Rt 6 and Rt 6a. At 0.3 mi you take a L fork and at 0.6 mi reach a parking lot and the end of the bicycle trail mentioned in the hike from Truro. Continue straight ahead (NE) on a sand road (open to dune buggies and hikers) 0.5 mi to a fork. The R fork leads immediately to the beach; the L fork (marked "emergency route") leads through the meadows, roughly paralleling the beach. Go to the beach, walk L (NW) for about 2.0 mi and watch for a break in the low dunes, blocked off from dune buggy access by a snow fence (1981). Go through the break and you will see first, the largest dune on the Cape 0.8 mi away to the S and second, the emergency route coming in from the L to a buggy track crossroad. Your way is straight ahead S across the emergency route (pass through a locked buggy barrier and follow a buggy track toward the great dunes). Leave the track when it nears the highest dune, and go R, climbing to the dune's top for its magnificent panoramic view. SW is Provincetown harbor, E is Pilgrim Lake and the Meadows and W is more of the dune country. From the dune top go SE down to a parking lot (not visible from the top) at the W end of Pilgrim Lake, just off Rt 6. Cross Rd 6 (carefully) to a sand path going over to Rt 6a. The motels listed are on Rt 6a and can be seen when you reach that road.

EAST—In the reverse direction, the access to the ocean beach is not marked. From the high dune near the Great Dunes parking lot you will see a dune buggy track going toward the ocean and ending at a break in the last low sand ridge before the water. The track is marked by pairs of posts, and you will see them marching across the slope of a dune to the S. You can reach the track at any one of these posts. Take the track to the beach, turn R (E) and follow in reverse the directions from High Head and Pilgrim Lake.

INLAND WALK THROUGH THE DUNES, WEST—At the fork in the buggy track just before High Head, take the signposted emergency route L rather than the beach access track. It will be slow going through soft sand, but you can rest by stopping to observe the dune vegetation. In about 2.0 mi a beach-access track blocked by a fence intersects your path. Go L on this track, through a locked buggy barrier, and follow the track to the Great Dunes parking area.

PROVINCETOWN VIA CAPE RACE BY BEACH—If you have fallen in love with beach walking, you can continue W along the beach from High Point to Cape Race Beach and thence inland to the middle of Provincetown. This adds another 5.5 mi to the day's hike, 4.0 mi of which are along the beach. We have not walked it, but the map shows no beach exit until Race Point Beach, a heavily used public beach and thus easily identified. From the beach parking lot a paved bicycle path paralleling Race Point Rd, leads most of the way into Provincetown. You will pass Province Lands Visitor Center, which has different exhibits from Salt Pond Visitor Center and is worth a stop.

Great Dune

HOUSATONIC WALK
Connecticut, 4 days, 41.9 miles (67.6 km)

SECTION	DISTANCE		OVERNIGHT POINTS
1	8.1 mi	(13.1 km)	Bulls Bridge-Kent
2	9.4 mi	(15.2 km)	Kent-Cornwall Bridge
3	9.5 mi	(15.3 km)	Cornwall Bridge-Tyler Lake
4	14.9 mi	(24.0 km)	Tyler Lake-Rt 7 (nr Falls Village)

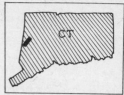

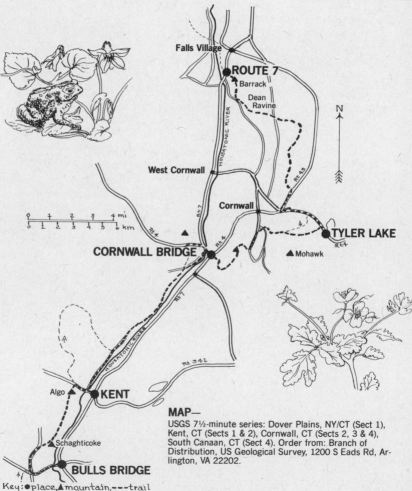

Falls Village

ROUTE 7

Barrack

Dean Ravine

HOUSATONIC RIVER

N

West Cornwall

Rt 43

Cornwall

Rt 7

TYLER LAKE

Rt 4

Rt 4

0 1 2 3 4 mi
0 1 2 3 4 5 6 km

Rt 4

CORNWALL BRIDGE

Rt 4

Mohawk

Rt 7

HOUSATONIC RIVER

Rt 341

Algo

KENT

Schaghticoke

BULLS BRIDGE

Key:●place,▲mountain,---trail

MAP—
USGS 7½-minute series: Dover Plains, NY/CT (Sect 1), Kent, CT (Sects 1 & 2), Cornwall, CT (Sects 2, 3 & 4), South Canaan, CT (Sect 4). Order from: Branch of Distribution, US Geological Survey, 1200 S Eads Rd, Arlington, VA 22202.

TRANSPORTATION
Bulls Bridge, Kent,
Cornwall Bridge, Rt 7—bus (Bonanza) NYC & Albany 3 r/t dly

ACCOMMODATIONS (area code 203)
Kent, CT 06757
    Candlelight Guest House   927-3407

Cornwall Bridge, CT 06754
    Bonney Brook Motel   672-6219
    Elm Motor Lodge   672-0005

Tyler Lake, Goshen, CT 06756
    Litchfield Hills Motel   491-3036

Rt 7, Falls Village, CT 06031
    Village Cabins and Restaurant   824-7886

Bulls Bridge—restaurant only (Bulls Bridge Inn)

Canoe Rentals on the Housatonic River—Riverrunning Expeditions, Ltd, Main St., Falls Village, CT 06031, tel. 824-5579

This Walk in western Connecticut covers a good portion of the wooded ridges, peaks and the river valley of the Housatonic Range. It starts at one of the last covered bridges in the state, crosses the Housatonic River, swings briefly into New York and goes north by the ridge west of the river to Kent, a charming river village. From here it takes an easy day along the west bank of the Housatonic by dirt roads and footpaths to Cornwall Bridge. It then leaves the river valley and goes east over Mohawk Mountain to Tyler Lake. The last day is a long but not too arduous trek back to the river just below Falls Village, with the dark gem of Dean Ravine and the steep pitches of Barrack Mountain to entertain you. The footing ranges from dirt roads and easy woods paths to

95

the rocks of the Giant Staircase and Barrack Mountain. There are frequent hemlock groves to temper the day's heat and to hush your footsteps. The way is nearly all wooded, but evidences of early farming are seen in old walls, stone heaps and cellar holes, and traces of early industry are left in the numerous charcoal-burning circles, where wood was burned in dirt-covered mounds to make charcoal. There are frequent viewpoints from the ledges and summits over which you pass. Going north, you have the option of returning by canoe (see p 99).

OVERNIGHT POINTS

Kent is a charming village, with attractive houses set in wide lawns. It has interesting shops and several good restaurants. The Sloan-Stanley Museum, with a display of colonial tools and other early artifacts, is at the north end of the village (Wed-Sun 10-4:30, Memorial Day-Oct). The well-known Kent School is across the river. The village was early a center of activity, with forges and grist, fulling and saw mills powered by a nearby brook. A tannery, brickyard, blacksmith shop and other trades also served the surrounding farms. **Cornwall Bridge** is a hamlet of a few houses by a now-modern bridge. There is a post office, general store and two motels. **Tyler Lake** is a summer colony, remarkable only for the beauty of the setting. The motel is high above the lake, with views north and south.

Bulls Bridge

1. BULLS BRIDGE—KENT
8.1 mi (13.1 km)/1630 ft (497 m)

This section introduces you to the high western ridge that forms one of the confines of the Housatonic River. You climb over two mountain summits before descending to the village of Kent. There are a number of good viewpoints toward the river and the ridges to the east and you pass several charcoal-burning circles en route, level, still-black circles on the forest floor. You will encounter a covered bridge; Rattlesnake Den, a gloomy ravine reputed to be infested with snakes (in which we found one small salamander!); Dry Gulch, a deep slash in the rock; a mountain streamside path through great hemlocks; and the Giant Staircase, a steep boulder-strewn pitch. It is a challenging hike with much to keep you interested. The way is well marked, the footing poor to excellent.

NORTH—At Bulls Bridge walk W off Rt 7 at the traffic light on a paved road going over a canal and through the covered bridge spanning the Housatonic River. The river here is rarely more than a jumble of rocks since it is below a dam and canal feeding a hydro-electric plant downstream. In 0.4 mi the river road goes R. If you feel the weather is too foul for ridge walking, take this pleasant, level 5.0-mi walk along the river, through woods and by an Indian reservation to Kent. Otherwise, continue straight ahead. At 1.4 mi you come to signposted Dog Tail Corner Rd (strange name!). Go R, picking up the white blazes of the Appalachian Trail (AT) on what becomes the SE Mt Rd at the R fork. This road passes a straggle of small houses and becomes a narrow dirt road which climbs steadily through woods.

At 2.9 mi the AT goes R uphill on a woods road. In a short distance go L on another woods road and climb by easy stages to the broad summit of Schaghticoke Mt, crossing one stream and passing a level spot with a charcoal-burning circle, now used as a campground. From the summit, continue on a ridge to the New York/Connecticut state line at 4.1 mi. There is a register here, so please sign in. From the state line you cross the ridge and soon reach Indian Rocks, extensive ledges on the E side of the mountain with good views across the river to the hills beyond. The last ledge, with the widest view, is North Point.

pitcher plant

You now begin to descend across the E slope of the mountain. At 4.5 mi cross Dry Gulch, a steep-sided ravine that looks more difficult to negotiate than it is. There is a trail at the bottom of this ravine which goes R down to the Schaghticoke Indian burial ground on the river road (signposted "closed" in 1981). Beyond the gulch continue your downward course and look for the ominous-sounding Rattlesnake Den. At 4.8 mi you come upon it, a boulder-strewn ravine with large hemlocks that reduce the illumination to a gloomy twilight. Why any self-respecting snake would live in that damp gloom, we can't imagine. Cross gingerly, to be on the safe side. Beyond a woods road leads you down to what was once a flat meadow, now largely rewooded. (Do not stray off the blazed route here as it is private land and the owner objects to trespass.) At 5.9 mi you reach another woods road running E-W between tumbled stone walls. Go L (W), enter a grove of hemlocks and cross Thayer Brook. Next you ascend through mature hemlocks high on the side of the deep Thayer ravine. Regretfully, you must leave the hemlocks, enter a deciduous forest and climb to the flat summit of Mt Algo (6.7 mi). You cross the summit by a path that soon goes downhill, gently at first and then precipitously at the end, around and down the boulders of the Giant Staircase to the river road at 7.4 mi. Take care going down this last pitch, as the rocks may be slippery. Go L on the river road to Rt 341 and R across the river to Kent. The Candlelight Guest House is L on Rt 7.

SOUTH—From the traffic light in Kent, walk W on Rt 341, cross the river and take the second road L (white blazes here). Go about 0.2 mi to a rocky path R going up Mt Algo. The remaining distances are summit of Mt Algo 1.4 mi; Rattlesnake Den 3.3 mi; Dry Gulch 3.6 mi; state line 4.0 mi; SE Mt Rd 5.2 mi; Dog Tail Corner 6.7 mi. The last point is the first crossroad after the paving begins and is signposted. Go L 1.4 mi to the traffic light on Rt 7 at Bulls Bridge. The bus will stop here on signal. There is an inn at this crossroad if you need a meal (no lodging).

bob-white

2. KENT—CORNWALL BRIDGE
9.4 mi (15.2 km)/level

This is an easy, level hike along the Housatonic River, partly on quiet dead-end roads and partly on paths. While the way is mostly through woods, you will pass small farms sandwiched between the river and the mountains. On the river there may be canoeists paddling with the current or a Kent school shell, its crew practicing for their next race.

It is the river which gives this day's trek its charm. Whether you are sitting on its bank enjoying a break or looking across it to the farms and hills beyond as you walk along an open part or merely feeling it beside you through the cover of the woods as the path bends slightly away, it is your constant near companion.

The river is generally placid, but near Cornwall Bridge there is a set of rapids, a favorite spot for a canoe slalom course. A half-dozen canoes were repeatedly shooting the rapids the day we passed and were being pulled back upstream along the water's edge to go through again. They reminded us that, at the end of the Walk, we were canoeing down the river to our starting point. Falls Village has a canoe outfitter who for a moderate fee takes care of the canoes at each end (see p 95), thus providing our walk-paddle option. Isn't this better than the fly-drive offered by the airlines? The river is lively enough to make paddling easy, but not so lively that a tyro canoeist cannot go down safely.

NORTH—Walk W on Rt 341 from the traffic light in Kent, cross the river and go R (N) on the river road. At 1.5 mi from the light the pavement ends and you soon cross a small bridge with a little waterfall L. At 3.1 mi the AT comes in from the L and you follow white blazes a short distance. In another mile you pass the remains of Swift's Bridge which once spanned the Housatonic. The AT goes L here, but you continue ahead. The road soon ends for autos at 4.3 mi but continues, much deteriorated, past a regimented plantation of pines. It finally peters out to a path that wanders through meadows and woods along the river to a paved road at 7.9 mi. The slalom rapids are here. Follow the road to Cornwall Bridge. It passes under the river bridge at 9.3 mi and reaches Rt 7 just beyond. Walk L (S) on Rt 7 across the bridge to the village. The Elm is just N (R) of the turnoff on Rt 7; the Bonney Brook is a short distance S of the post office on Rt 7.

SOUTH—Walk N from Cornwall Bridge Village on Rt 7 across the bridge and go R on Rt 7 to first road R (River Rd). Go S on this road for 1.5 mi until it swings away from the river, and take the path along the river to a dirt and then paved road leading to Rt 341. Go L to Kent.

wooden gothic
at Cornwall Bridge

3. CORNWALL BRIDGE—TYLER LAKE
9.5 mi (15.3 km) / 1026 ft (313 m)

In this hike you see best that distinctive combination of the Connecticut pastoral lowland nestling against the wooded mountains. You follow the Appalachian Trail most of the way, over the high ridge of Coltsfoot Mountain with its open ledges and down through the Dudleytown valley, with its picture-perfect red barns and neat fields. From the valley you climb through Cathedral Pines, a protected stand of gigantic white pines, to the long ridge of Mohawk Mountain, skirting the tops of ski slopes. There is a nature bog to visit and a quiet country road to carry you down to Tyler Lake.

We made this trip after a day-long torrential rainstorm in early May, so the woods were newly washed and the waterfalls plunged down in their full glory. The rains also had brought forth newts too numerous to count—newts of various sizes, from a half inch to three inches long, showing their bright red suits as they sunned themselves on the dark earth or on silver green rocks at our feet. It was as if it had rained newts as well as raindrops the night before. We commented on how lucky we were not to have any small children with us. If we had we never would have made it through the area by sundown, since we have yet to meet the small child able to pass by a little red newt. Still, we would have liked to watch one of our own young naturalists responding to this plenitude of creatures.

EAST—From the Cornwall Bridge post office, cross the junction of Rts 7 and 4 to a narrow paved road going E uphill (Dark Entry Rd) and picking up the blazes of the AT. The way soon turns to dirt and becomes a private road. At 1.0 mi the road turns R and in 100 yds you go L on an old woods road across a stream (Bonney Brook) and along its S bank. The stream here is a series of cascades and waterfalls in a stand of hemlocks. Just past the remains of an old dam, you cross the stream (hemlocks here as much as 3 ft in diameter). At 1.5 mi you leave the hemlocks, cross a woods road into a second-growth forest and ascend the E slope of Coltsfoot Mt up and along attractive ledges to Echo Rock, with good views E (2.8 mi). Descend over rough ground to the base of the mountain. At 3.6 mi a blue-blazed trail leads R 0.2 mi to Dudley's Caves, formed by a fall of enormous boulders. One cave is reached by a short climb, the second is at the base of the boulder field a little farther on (a flashlight here is an asset).

From the side trail junction you descend to the paved Dudleytown Rd; go L through a gradually opening farm valley to a trail going R into the woods by a giant white pine (double white blazes, 5.2 mi). The charming village of Cornwall, 0.5 mi down Dudleytown Rd, is worth a short visit if you have the energy. From the road you climb steeply through a magnificent stand of white

pines, well named Cathedral Pines. You soon cross a paved road and continue climbing through the pines, now in a nature sanctuary which preserves the old trees. The forest floor here is a deep carpet of needles, with the only greenery being ferns, partridge berries, vines and some mosses. The big white pines gradually give way to smaller trees, still predominantly evergreen.

The trail joins an old woods road which comes in on the L, dips down beside a farm (L) and ends at paved Essex Hill Rd. Turn L to its intersection with Great Hollow Rd and go R. At the first fork, go L into a private drive leading close beside a house. Cross a small wood bridge and climb up a grassy track between two stone walls, with a field and orchard on your L. The way becomes a telephone line right of way. At an intersection of two stone walls you may be confused by white blazes R, but these mark a boundary. Your way is straight ahead, with white blazes of the AT leading you steeply uphill through woods. There is a stream L which you cross in a slight dip. In a short time you reach a broad ski trail; go R on this trail uphill and bear L at an open spot to a stone tower and the top of a chair lift (excellent views of the valley below). Pass in front of the chair lift and take a path R, signposted "To Timbers." At the next fork head "To Timbers" again and pass in front of a second chair lift. Turn R and soon reach paved Tomey Rd by an overlook (another good view of the valley). The way is well blazed even if the trail description sounds complicated. Leave the AT here and go directly across Tomey Rd to a woods road with a chain across (no blazes), to the R of the AT. Follow the woods road, going L at a fork, to Allyn Rd opposite the buildings of the Park headquarters. To the R a nature trail through a bog is worth a small digression. Go L (E) on Allyn Rd down the mountain 1.5 mi to Rt 4. The Litchfield Hills Motel is 0.4 mi R, high on a hill overlooking Tyler Lake.

WEST—Walk W on Rt 4 from the Litchfield Hills Motel to Allyn Rd. Go L 1.5 mi to a trail R, opposite the Park headquarters. Follow this trail, going R at a fork, to join the AT (white blazes) at a paved road and overlook. Go L on the AT, past the tops of two chair lifts and down to Dudleytown Rd in the valley bottom (4.3 mi). Go L 1.5 mi on this road and R into the woods just beyond where the open fields end. This path takes you over Coltsfoot Mt to a dirt road leading R down to Cornwall Bridge.

4. TYLER LAKE—RT 7 (NR FALLS VILLAGE)
14.9 mi (24.0 km) / 1200 ft (366 m)
This section starts out mundanely on forest paths (if going north), but it becomes increasingly varied and interesting until it reaches its climax of beauty and excitement going down Dean Ravine and up and down Barrack Mountain. The walk through the Ravine is spectacular, featuring a cascading brook that tumbles through a high rocky cut. The ferns and mosses nurtured by these falling waters make the setting a green fairyland, while the absorption of all sound save the roar of the waterfall creates a feeling surprisingly akin to that evoked by deep silence, one of peace and awe. The challenging climb up the rocks and ledges of Barrack Mountain is rewarded by the excellent views. Unless you do this hike out of season you will be accompanied up and down Barrack by a mechanical sound which is foreign to the natural setting. It begins as you climb the south slope as a sort of bee hum and increases in volume until, when you descend the north slope, the sound will reach an unbelievable level. It is the whine of auto racers at the Lime Rock Race Track miles away. The phenomenon surprisingly does not detract from the pleasure of the hike because it comes to you from another world.

Deanes Ravine

NORTH—Walk W (on Rt 4) from the Litchfield Hills Motel for 1.5 mi to the AT crossing (double white blazes), and go R into the woods. The path soon turns downhill and delivers you back on Rt 4 0.5 mi W of where you left it. Turn R (W) on Rt 4 to a junction with Rt 43, 2.8 mi from the motel. Go R on Rt 43 1.1 mi, and opposite Indian Ln take a woods road L (W). Ascend in 0.5 mi by an easy gradient to the broad top of Overlook Mt (1428 ft), and then descend to a ledge at 4.6 mi, with views E. Beyond, follow the broad wooded ridge with little change of elevation, and finally descend through a handsome birch-pine woods to cross paved Lake Rd at 5.9 mi. The next 1.5 mi is by easy paths and woods roads up and along Pond Hill. At 7.5 mi cross the dirt Ford Hill Rd and pass through a small plantation of tall thin pines which look ready for the telephone-pole market.

Climb gradually, cross the broad top of Yelping Hill ridge and descend over rocky terrain to an old beaver pond at 8.7 mi (go R to look at the pond and its drowned trees). In about 0.2 mi you will see a gravel road ahead (Mt Titus Rd); parallel this road until you descend to and skirt a man-made pond to its dam. Follow the overflow down to the gravel Mansfield Rd (9.2 mi). Cross and follow the stream a short distance before skirting a large swamp on your R for 0.5 mi to gravel W Yelping Hill Rd. Cross over to go up a forest maintenance road along the top of a ridge, with glimpses of views to the R. At an old picnic table turn sharply R and gradually descend, crossing several brooks, to a small clearing bisected by Wickwire Rd, which is grassy and unused L and graveled to the R (10.3 mi). Go R, seemingly in the direction from which you have come. At 11.1 mi leave the road and turn R on a lesser-used grassy forest road which crosses a woods road in a sag, ascends slightly and narrows. At 11.9 mi go R, descend steeply by switchbacks on good footing through a pine forest until you reach a brook. Cross the brook and follow its W bank to paved Music Mt

Rd by a waterfall. Cross the road to a path down through Dean Ravine. The way is as beautiful as it is billed, past waterfalls and cascades.

In all too short a time you are through the ravine and back on Music Mt Rd. Go R on the road a short way to a path R up a steep bank just after the road crosses a small bridge. A short climb brings you to a rocky outcrop where you get your first of many views. You will now work for these views as the way is steep and the footing rough, and you will need an occasional assist from a hand or two. It is time-consuming rather than difficult, as you carefully pick your way. After the first rise of land and a small sag, the way is even steeper and rockier until you reach the edge of an escarpment. Looking back you get views of the near valley and far hills, while ahead are the ledges you will soon climb. When you gain the top of these ledges (14.3 mi) you are at Lookout Point; the vista over the Housatonic Valley is ample reward for your efforts. From here you dip down and climb a short way to the real summit of Barrack Mt, clothed in trees. You come out on North Rock at 14.6 mi, with the sight of the river and a regional high school below. You now go down a path fully as steep and rough as the one you went up. It ends at Rt 7 just by the Village Cabins and Restaurant. You can catch the bus here or stay the night at the Cabins if, the following day, you want to go into Falls Village to rent a canoe for a restful return trip downriver (see p 95).

SOUTH—Walk S from the Valley Cabins on Rt 7 to the white-blazed AT going L (E) uphill. Follow this to Rt 43 and go R to Rt 4; turn L on Rt 4 and go 0.4 mi to a parallel path. This returns you to Rt 4 in 0.5 mi; you leave the AT and go L 1.5 mi to the Litchfield Hills Motel. The mileages are North Rock 0.8 mi; Lookout Point 1.0 mi; W Yelping Hill Rd 5.3 mi; Ford Hill Rd 7.4 mi; Lake Rd 9.0 mi; Rt 43 11.0 mi; Rt 4 12.1 mi; leave AT at 13.4 mi.

HIGH PEAKS WALK
New York, 4 day circuit, 29.6 miles (47.7 km)

SECTION	DISTANCE	OVERNIGHT POINTS
1	8.1 mi (13.1 km)	Keene Valley-Johns Brook Lodge
2	6.9 mi (11.1 km)	Johns Brook Lodge-Heart Lake via Klondike Notch
3	5.9 mi (9.5 km)	Heart Lake-South Meadow Farm Lodge
4	8.7 mi (14.0 km)	South Meadow Farm Lodge-Keene Valley
2a	13.0 mi (21.0 km)	Johns Brook Lodge-Heart Lake via Mt Marcy
4a	9.6 mi (15.5 km)	South Meadow Farm Lodge-Keene

MAP—
ADK Map Adirondack High Peaks Region.
Order from Adirondack Mt Club, RD 1,
Ridge Rd, Glen Falls, NY 12801.

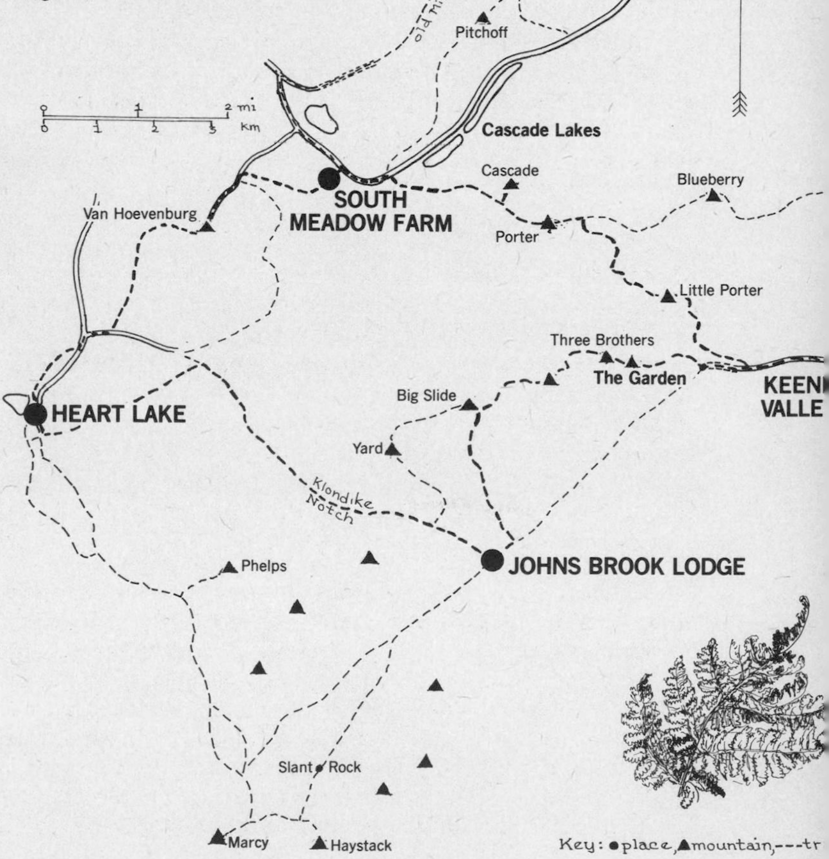

NY

KEENE

Rt 73

old military road

Pitchoff

Cascade Lakes

0 1 2 mi
0 1 2 3 km

Cascade

Blueberry

Van Hoevenburg

SOUTH MEADOW FARM

Porter

Little Porter

Three Brothers

Big Slide

The Garden

KEENE VALLE

HEART LAKE

Yard

Klondike Notch

Phelps

JOHNS BROOK LODGE

Slant Rock

Marcy   Haystack

Key: ●place, ▲mountain, ---tr

106

TRANSPORTATION
Keene Valley—bus (Adirondack Trailways)—Albany & NYC
 3 r/t dly

Keene—taxi or limousine—Saranac Lake/Lake Placid airport

South Meadow Farm Lodge—air (US Air, Air North)

ACCOMMODATIONS (area code 518)
Keene Valley, NY 12943
 Spread Eagle Inn   576-9986

Keene, NY 12942
 Barkeater Lodge   576-2221

Lake Placid, NY 12946
 Johns Brook Lodge, PO Box 867   523-3441
 Adirondak Loj, PO Box 867   523-3441
 South Meadow Farm Lodge   523-9369

This is a sampling of the many hikes in the high peaks region of the Adirondack Mountains. It uses the comfortable lodges of the Adirondack Mountain Club (ADK) and attractive country inns. The basic route is a circuit that begins and ends in the village of Keene Valley. There are alternate sections: a strenuous day's climb over Mt Marcy, New York's highest mountain, and a route along an unused road that can be done in all seasons. The basic route climbs from Keene Valley over the summits of four mountains, with a half mile of ledge walking, down to the remote Johns Brook Lodge, thence through a high notch to the Adirondak Loj

Johns Brook Lodge

at Heart Lake, returning over another mountain, by a country inn and two more mountains to Keene Valley. You will go over seven peaks in all, three over 4000 feet and each giving magnificent views of the surrounding wilderness. You will cover all the climatic zones of the Adirondacks, from the mixed deciduous forest of the valleys, through pure birch woods to the mixed birch-conifers of the high peaks.

The basic route (Sections 1-4) can be hiked only in the summer months because the Johns Brook Lodge is only open July 1 to Labor Day. When it is closed, you can still hike into the lodge along Johns Brook on the shorter and easier Northside Trail (5.2 miles) and then go on to do Section 2, all in one day (12.1 miles in all of fairly easy hiking). When the high peaks are covered with snow, we suggest replacing Section 4 (Cascade and Porter mountains) with Section 4a, an old military road ending at Keene rather than at Keene Valley. For the strong hikers, Section 2 can be replaced by Section 2a, a climb over Mt Marcy. This is a more strenuous hike than we normally include (13 miles, 3100 feet elevation gain) but can be done by anyone in good physical condition. (If the summits are in clouds it may not be worth the effort, unless you simply want to bag New York's highest peak.)

OVERNIGHT POINTS

Keene Valley is a quiet village deep in the Adirondacks. It is a hiking center for the many peaks that surround it and has a small number of summer as well as year-round residents. **Johns Brooks Lodge**, owned by the Adirondack Mountain Club (ADK) and built in 1925, is a single rustic building on the west bank of the Johns Brook, five miles from Keene Valley and three miles by trail from an auto road. It has dormitory sleeping. (Blankets and pillows are provided, but you must bring a sheet bag.) It offers ample family-style meals, hot water showers and congenial company. Trail lunches are provided. The main room has a cheerful fireplace, books and the memorabilia of hikes and hikers. It is open from July 1 to Labor Day. The ADK has two cabins close by, used during the other months, but there you must pack in and cook your own food. **Heart Lake** is a small gem of water five miles off Rt 73, east of Lake Placid. There is a complex of shelters, tent spaces, a hikers building and the Adirondak Loj, operated by the ADK. The Loj, well situated by the lake, has all the comforts of a good inn, and its clientele are mostly hikers. You can swim and fish in Heart Lake or take some of the many day hikes from the lodge, including some led by naturalists. There is a network of cross-country ski and snowshoe trails to enjoy in the winter. **South Meadow Farm Lodge** is an inn a short way off the Lake Placid Road (Rt 73), a half mile east of the Mt Hoevenberg Winter Sports Complex entrance. It is a working farm, attractively sited in a field backed by woods, catering especially to hikers and skiers. **Keene** is an even smaller village than Keene Valley and is located five miles north of it at the junction of Rts 73 and 9N. If you hike Section 4a, we suggest that you stay at the Barkeater Lodge, an inn in an old farmhouse, also catering to hikers and skiers. It has a cross-country ski center where equipment and instruction may be obtained in the snow months.

Second Brother

1. KEENE VALLEY—JOHNS BROOK LODGE
8.1 mi (13.1 km)/2800 ft (850 m)

This section is a marvelous introduction to the Adirondack High Peak Region. It has more ledge walking than any other trail, with constant views of the surrounding peaks and valleys. You climb by road from the quiet village of Keene Valley to the Garden, and then take the Brothers Trail over the Three Brothers peaks and Big Slide Mountain with its imposing south cliff plunging from the summit. You end at the rustic but comfortable Johns Brook

Lodge, reachable only by foot. The trail has great variety—bare
ledges, great birch forests (some of the trees large enough to make
a birchbark canoe), cascading brooks and trail footing varying
from soft pine needles to sheets of living rock. The way is well
marked, the footing poor to good.

SOUTHWEST—In Keene Valley, take the paved road W from Rt
73, just by the Spread Eagle Inn, signposted "Trail to the High
Peaks." Follow the yellow markers. At 0.6 mi you cross Johns
Brook on an iron bridge and begin to climb steadily. The road
becomes dirt and ends at a small parking lot known as the Garden
(1.6 mi). Go to its W end. There is an easy trail (the Northside
Trail) to Johns Brook Lodge, which follows the W bank of the
brook, leaving by the bulletin board (be sure to register). You,
however, will be going via the Brothers Trail, which leaves a few
yds to the R, red blazed. The trail climbs by easy stages at first
through a mixed forest and then through white birches. About
0.5 mi from the Garden the trail steepens; you soon reach the first
of a series of rock ledges, with good views of Hurricane (NE),
Giant and the Range (E) and Johns Brook and Marcy (SW). You
then climb for 0.5 mi, mostly on ledges, dividing your attention
between the views and the footing, until the grade slackens and
you reach the bare ridge. The flat rocks of the summit of First
Brother (2940 ft) are reached 3.0 mi from Keene Valley. From the
summit you can now look N to Porter and Cascade mts and ahead
to the other Brothers.

Still on bare rock you dip briefly before climbing to Second
Brother (3120 ft) 0.2 mi beyond. Now, alas, you leave the views
and enter the forest; descend slightly and then climb steadily
through white birch until you come out on the summit of Third
Brother (3681 ft, 4.1 mi). Here you get a profile of the great slide
on Big Slide Mt, a nearly perpendicular wall of rock, as well as
good views of Noonmark, Dix Peak, Nipple Top, the Range and
the Haystacks.

From the summit of the Third Brother descend into a spruce-
balsam forest whose floor is covered with ferns, pass a natural rock
shelter L and reach a col at 4.7 mi. From the col climb steadily but
easily to the junction with the Slide Mt Brook Trail at 5.1 mi. Big
Slide Mt (4240 ft) is 500 yds to the R, a steep scramble up rocks
and slippery dirt. The top is wooded, but the cliff edge of the
slide affords marvelous views of Giant, Dix Peak, the Great
Range, Mt Colden and the MacIntyre Mts. The views are well
worth the struggle up.

Return to the trail junction and go S down the red-blazed Slide Mt Brook Trail. About 1.0 mi from the trail junction you follow a brook, which you will cross and recross a number of times. At 1.5 mi from the junction you go down a long bare rock slide. At 7.8 mi from Keene Valley (including the climb up Big Slide Mt), you reach the Phelps or Northside Trail coming up from the Garden. Go R on Phelps (yellow blazes) 0.3 mi to the Johns Brook Lodge.

NORTHEAST—Leave Johns Brook Lodge at its NE end and take the trail toward Keene Valley (yellow blazes). At 0.3 mi take the Slide Mt Brook Trail L (red blazed). The mileages from the lodge are junction with the Brothers Trail 2.4 mi; Big Slide Mt 2.7 mi; return to junction 3.0 mi; Third Brother 4.0 mi; Second Brother 4.8 mi; First Brother 5.1 mi; the Garden 6.5 mi.

Heart Lake

2. JOHNS BROOK LODGE—HEART LAKE VIA KLONDIKE NOTCH

6.9 mi (11.1 km)1127 ft (345 m) W, 886 ft (265 m) E

This is an enjoyable, easy, wooded hike over the Klondike Notch, between the two Adirondack Mountain Club lodges. There is a stretch on a cross-country ski trail that winds through woods and meadows, in summer a profusion of flowering weeds that lend bright color to your day. The meadows are open enough for glimpses of the surrounding peaks. The brook down from the notch called to mind a scene here of some years ago that still makes us smile. Although early spring, it was a sweltering day. We thought to cool off in one of the deep pools, so we stripped and stepped in. The water was bitterly cold and we retreated. Suddenly we found we were about to have company and in a fit of proper

Marcy Brook

modesty plunged in, the gentleman to the waist, the lady to the neck. The hiker courteously stopped, and we politely exchanged pleasantries for what seemed like an eternity. Without ever changing expression he tipped his hat and went on his way. Before we emerged we looked down at ourselves. Through the crystal clear water we stood clearly revealed! So much for modesty. The notch is not high, the way is well marked and the footing generally good. There are a few boggy places, especially in the meadows.

WEST—From the SW end of the John Brooks Lodge, take the red-blazed Klondike Notch Trail R (NW). It crosses and climbs along the bank of the Black Brook until near the top of the notch. The grade is moderate, with a number of level bits to ease the going. At 1.3 mi the Yard Mt-Big Slide Trail goes R. Your trail goes straight ahead uphill, crossing a level swampy area and then climbing again through a spruce forest. You reach the height of land in the Klondike Notch at 1.7 mi, drop down to a sag and shortly cross another divide. From here the trail descends at easy to moderate grades, crosses Klondike Brook at 2.6 mi and reaches the Klondike Dam lean-to at 2.7 mi. Pass in front of the lean-to (but do not cross the brook), and climb briefly to reach the remains of an old woods road. You go W along this road, climbing a bit at first but then going by easy grades down to the wooded flat before the South Meadow. The road is eroded in spots but generally improves as you progress.

At 4.8 mi the Mr Van Ski Trail goes R to the Mt Van Hoevenberg bobsled run and X-C ski trails In 0.2 mi the Mr Van Ski Trail goes L. Take this trail. It is blazed red at infrequent intervals and in summer is overgrown with weeds. However, the way is clear underfoot and the line of the trail will be indicated by the lack of trees. The distance from here to the Adirondak Loj is 1.9 mi (sign here in 1981 said 0.9 mi) on level trail through woods and meadows. In 0.5 mi you cross the gravel truck road to Marcy Dam and in another 0.5 mi cross Marcy Brook on a new wood bridge (very boggy through the meadow here). Beyond the brook you enter a pine woods (the red discs are joined by blue paint blazes). You reach the Van Hoevenberg Trail to Mt Marcy (blue discs) 0.8 mi from Marcy Brook. There is no signpost here. Go R on this trail a short distance to the hikers' parking lot, and follow the signs to the lodge.

EAST—From the Adirondak Loj go out to the S end of the hikers' parking lot and take the blue-blazed trail to Marcy Dam and Mt Marcy. In a short distance Mr Van Trail (not signposted) crosses the Marcy trail. Go L, following red discs and blue blazes (the latter die out at the bridge). At 1.9 mi you reach the Klondike Notch Trail. Go R and climb over the notch to Johns Brook Lodge.

from Van Hoevenberg

3. HEART LAKE—SOUTH MEADOW LODGE
5.9 mi (9.5 km) / 740 ft (226 m)

This is a very easy day by cross-country ski trails and a path that takes you over the ledges and past the famous bobsled and luge runs of Mt Van Hoevenberg. From the moutain ledges you will get a view of the entire four-day Walk, from Cascade and Porter mountains around to the long ridge of the Brothers and Big Slide and the distinctive Klondike Notch. Mts Marcy and Algonquin will be in the background. Below you will see the marshes and meadows of the South Meadow Brook.

You will enjoy seeing and even walking on the bobsled and luge runs on Van Hoevenberg. The bobsled run is the only one of its kind in North America, the luge one of two. They differ principally in the type of sled used. The bobsleds are two- and four-person heavy steel affairs with steering and brake mechanisms. The luge is a single-person sled of wood, braked and steered with the feet. Neither look particularly safe, and the vertically banked turns of their runs look dangerous even on a bright summer day. The small

museum at the bottom of the runs is worth a short visit to learn more about Olympic sledding. Lunch or refreshments can be purchased in the restaurant underneath. The cross-country ski trails you use are part of the Olympic biathalon course, a curious race on skis involving stopping to shoot at targets—no doubt an offshoot of mountaineering warfare.

NORTHEAST—Walk around the E side of the Adirondak Loj on a dirt road going past the small Loj Nature Center. Just by the Center is a trail R signposted "Rimrock," marked with red discs and blue paint blazes. Follow this trail for 0.8 mi through an open deciduous forest with ferns as understory. The trail forks once and you take the R fork, soon going downhill to the paved Loj access road, which the trail has paralleled. Go L on the access road to a dirt road leading R to South Meadow. Take this road to the signposted trail (L) to Mt Van Hoevenberg (blazed blue), and head N on a level woods road in a red pine forest. It soon narrows to a single track and descends to a marshy area, with split logs over the boggiest parts. In about 1.0 mi you begin to climb through a mixed hardwood forest, with glimpses R that show you are on the edge of a ravine. You will pass high humps of rock on the L, not craggy but smooth like the backs of dinosaurs crouching by the trail. You go through a narrow defile and continue climbing easily until you reach open ledges R which give great views of South Meadow below and the entire arc of the Walk, from Cascade around to Marcy and the little hump of Mt Jo hard by Heart Lake. There is now a sequence of open ledges that leads you to the partly wooded summit of Mt Van Hoevenberg (2860 ft) at 3.3 mi.

Continuing N, drop down a moderate grade to an old road which once must have carried Victorian ladies to the summit. The road goes L to circle up to the summit, but you continue downhill. In 0.8 mi from the summit, you reach the top of the bobsled run. Here you have the choice of several routes to the bottom: the paved access road that carries the sleds and drivers up in winter; the dirt path beside the bobsled run; or, in summer, the run itself for a first-hand view of the banked curves. Partway down the luge run starts, a newer and more startling concrete snake. At 4.9 mi you reach the bottom of both runs at a museum and restaurant. Go out to the NE end of the parking lot and through the woods a short distance to a clearing and building. Here a number of X-C ski trails start. Go to the E end of the clearing and pick up a yellow-and-green blazed trail. There are numbered markers at all intersections; the first number you will see is 82. At 48 take the fork blazed yellow. About 1.0 mi from the bottom of the bobsled run, between markers 11 and 12, a sign points L (NE) to the nearby South Meadow Farm Lodge.

SOUTHWEST—Get directions from the South Meadow Farm Lodge on how to reach the yellow-blazed X-C ski trail. Go R on this trail until you reach marker 82. At the W end of the nearby building, follow the signs to the bobsled run parking area. Go to the bottom of the run and take either the paved access road or the path beside the bobsled run to its top. Here an old road and then trail (blue blazed) goes S over the summit of Mt Van Hoevenberg and down to a dirt road (4.7 mi). Go R 0.2 mi to a paved road and turn L. You soon cross a narrow bridge. Watch carefully on the R for a red-blazed X-C ski trail (not signposted) about 100 yds beyond the bridge. Take this trail about 1.0 mi to a dirt road leading L a short distance to the Adirondak Loj.

4. SOUTH MEADOW LODGE—KEENE VALLEY
8.7 mi (14.0 km) / 2700 ft (820 m)

This is a hike for the views, and you will hope for a clear day. You reach the top of two 4000-foot peaks and from their bare rock summits get spectacular vistas of all the other high peaks of the Adirondacks and even of the Green Mountains far to the east. The hike onto these two peaks is one of the most popular in the Adirondacks. It is a short, interesting trail with easy access to its base and has the kinds of views you get from the highest peak, Mt Marcy. Thus, on summer weekends you may have plenty of company on the way in, but the second half of the trip will be in solitude on little-used trails. The way is well marked, the footing good.

EAST—Walk E from South Meadow Farm Lodge on Rt 73 for 0.7 mi to a red-blazed trail R signposted to Cascade and Porter mts. The trail descends for a short distance and then climbs easily to a good-sized brook 0.3 mi from the road. Fill your canteens here as it is the last sure water until beyond Porter Mt. Beyond you pass huge old maples and climb steeply to a ridge. The grade moderates, and there are views of Big Slide, Marcy, Colden and Algonquin mts as you move along the ridge. At 2.8 mi you reach the side trail to Cascade Mt. If the day is clear the 0.2-mi, 300-ft climb to the summit is worth the effort. The way is mostly in the open and the top is bare rock. You can see in all directions. E is Lake Champlain, Camel's Hump and Mt Mansfield in Vermont. NW is the Cascade Lakes and Whiteface Mt, while S and SW are all the other major peaks of the Adirondacks. Returning to the junction, turn E and climb on a gentle grade to the bare summit of Porter Mt (4059 ft, 3.5 mi). Porter is much like Cascade yet not quite so panoramic.

From Porter you descend on a easy grade along a ridge, past the E summit, to a grassy area 0.4 mi from the main summit. Here there is a fork in the trail. Straight ahead carries you over Blueberry Mt to the small airport N of Keene Valley village; R goes to the village and is the route we describe. You descend steadily until a mile from Porter and then climb over several gentle rises. The last rise is Little Porter Mt (5.6 mi from the lodge), a bare promontory with views S and SW of Noonmark, Giant, the Range, Big Slide and the Brothers, the latter showing their bare backsides. You can see the village of Keene Valley, also. The little summit is a serene place and ideal for lunching.

Now you have 0.2 mi of bare ledge walking with little change of elevation, ending in a fitful descent to the valley. You will join a lumbering road briefly soon after the ledges and leave it at a cabin. Avoid a private trail R and cross a jeep road at 6.5 mi, with the site of a former maple sugar camp beyond. The trail forks 0.2 mi from the camp, and you go L, reaching the road to Keene Valley at 7.4 mi. Go L downhill to the village and Rt 73 at the Spread Eagle Inn.

WEST—From Rt 73 in Keene Valley take the road W from the Spread Eagle Inn. At 1.3 mi a trail, blazed red and signposted to Porter Mt, goes R. The mileages are Little Porter Mt 3.1 mi; Porter Mt 5.2 mi; trail junction to Cascade Mt 5.9 mi; Rt 73 8.0 mi. Go L on Rt 73 0.7 mi to the entrance road to the South Meadow Farm Lodge.

chipmunk

2a. JOHNS BROOK LODGE—HEART LAKE VIA MT MARCY

13.0 mi (21.0 km) / 3030 ft (920 m) W, 3165 ft (965 m) E
Mt Marcy is the center attraction for Adirondack hikers mostly because it is the highest peak in the region and indeed in the state. You will therefore see more hikers on this section than you will on any of the others. The views from the top of Marcy are well worth the long climb. On a clear day you can see a great portion of the Adirondack Preserve and east to the peaks of the Green Mountains in Vermont. The route uses two of the oldest trails in the region, the Phelps Trail from Johns Brook Lodge and the Van Hoevenberg Trail from Adirondak Loj. You will pass Slant Rock, a huge inclined slab that is a dramatic shelter from the elements. We spent a stormy night there when our children were very young. A cold wet wind howled over the rock, but the fire, reflected off the rock, kept us warm. It was a perfect setting for the tales we told of Indians on the warpath who once camped here.
WEST—Leave from the SW end of the John Brooks Lodge on the yellow-blazed trail going up the W bank of the brook. At 0.9 mi you pass Hogback lean-to, cross Hogback Brook and climb steeply up the hogback (a small, sharp ridge). The grade soon eases. At 1.5 mi a side trail goes L a short distance downhill to Bushnell Falls. At a junction beyond, the Hopkins Trail, blazed yellow, goes straight ahead, but you go L on Phelps, which now is red blazed. Cross the Johns Brook at 1.7 mi (if water is too high to cross here, go 100 yds upstream to footbridge).

The trail now climbs by easy stages to the great slab of Slant Rock (3.3 mi) and soon passes the yellow-blazed Shorey Short Cut L. The trail steepens, passing the blue-blazed Range Trail L at 4.3 mi, and finally moderates its grade at 4.9 mi. The Phelps Trail ends at 5.0 mi when it reaches the blue-blazed Van Hoevenberg Trail. Go L 0.6 mi to the summit of Marcy (5344 ft) on a route marked by paint on the bare rocks and by small cairns. In rain or fog take great care not to lose sight of these markers. Return from the summit by the same route and continue on the Van Hoevenberg Trail past the junction with the Phelps Trail (6.1 mi). At 6.5 mi the Hopkins Trail (yellow markers) and the Van Hoevenberg Bypass (red markers) come in on the R. Continue following the blue markers. At 7.9 mi the Van Hoevenberg Bypass returns R, and a red-blazed trail goes L to the Lake Arnold Trail. At 9.6 mi a red-blazed side trail goes R to Phelps Mt. Follow the blue blazes only. At 10.7 mi you reach Marcy Dam and the junction with the yellow-blazed trail to Avalanche Pass and Lake Colden. At 12.0 mi a yellow-blazed trail to Algonquin goes L, and at 13.0 mi you reach the hikers' parking lot at Heart Lake.

EAST—Leave the S end of the hikers' parking lot at Heart Lake by the blue-blazed Van Hoevenberg Trail. The mileages are Marcy Dam 2.3 mi; Phelps Mt Trail 3.4 mi; Hopkins Trail and Van Hoevenberg Bypass 6.5 mi; Phelps Trail 6.9 mi; Mt Marcy 7.5 mi; return to yellow-blazed Phelps Trail 8.1 mi; Range Trail 8.7 mi; Slant Rock 9.7 mi; Hopkins Trail 11.5 mi.

4a. SOUTH MEADOW LODGE—KEENE
9.6 mi (15.5 km)/320 ft (98 m) NE, 1370 ft (418 m) SW

In the event that Cascade and Porter mountains are impassible because of the weather, there is a hike over an old military road to

Slant Rock

Keene, five miles north of Keene Valley and served by the same bus line. The way is not blazed but is easy to follow. The footing is poor to good.

NORTHEAST—Go out the South Meadow Lodge access road, and go L on Rt 73. At 1.4 mi a dirt road goes R. It is about 0.5 mi beyond the entrance to the Mt Van Hoevenberg Sports Complex, the fourth and largest dirt road at a bend in Rt 73 after the entrance. This is the old military road (unmarked). The first 0.5 mi is passable by car, the next 0.5 mi by jeep, and then you tramp the unimproved remains of the old road. It trends NE and is a wide, sometimes eroded swath in the forest, not easy to wander from. At 3.1 mi from the lodge, you reach an active beaver pond which has flooded the old road. You will find a path of sorts on the L (NW) bank of the pond about 6 ft above the water. At 3.4 mi you reach the height of land (2350 ft) and begin the long descent to Keene. You pass several ponds, descend several steep sections and finally come out on a good dirt road (Alstead Mill Rd, 5.8 mi). It leads to the Barkeater Lodge at 8.3 mi and Rt 73 at 8.8 mi. Keene is 0.8 mi L.

SOUTHWEST—Walk W on Rt 73 from Keene 0.8 mi to Alstead Mill Rd (sign to Barkeater Lodge). Go R, passing the lodge, and continue to the end of the road; pick up a trail through the woods (the old military road) going in the same direction. When Rt 73 is reached again, turn L and go about 1.5 mi on Rt 73 to the South Meadow Farm Lodge sign. The mileages are end of Alstead Mill Rd 3.9 mi; height of land 6.3 mi; Rt 73 8.2 mi.

CATSKILLS WALK
New York, 3 days, 26.7 miles (43.1 km)

SECTION	DISTANCE		OVERNIGHT POINTS
1	5.4 mi	(8.7 km)	Big Indian-Pine Hill
2	10.2 mi	(16.5 km)	Pine Hill-Oliverea
3	11.1 mi	(17.9 km)	Oliverea-Shandaken

MAP—
Hikers Maps: No 67 NW Catskills (Sects 1 & 2), No 66 Central
Catskills (Sect 3) Order from Walking News, Inc., PO Box 352,
New York, NY 10013.

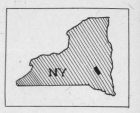

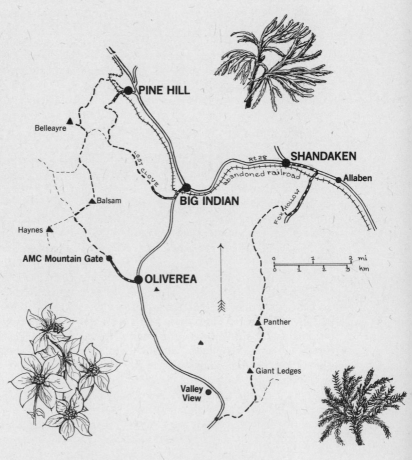

Key: ● place, ▲ mountain, --- trail

120

TRANSPORTATION
Big Indian, Pine Hill and Shandaken are all on the same Adirondack Trailways bus line—NYC via Kingston, 5 r/t daily (bus info 212-564-8484.)

ACCOMMODATIONS (area code 914)
Pine Hill, NY 12465

Pine Hill Arms	254-9811
White House Lodge	254-4200

Oliverea*, NY 12462

Mountain Gate Lodge (Appalachian Mtn. Club)	
open to public	254-4770
Valley View House Hotel	254-5117

Shandaken, NY 12480

Auberge Des 4 Saisons	688-2233

*see trail description for lodge and inn location

This Walk will dispel once and for all the image of the Catskills being only Grossingers and other lavish resorts. Located in the very heart of the Catskill Park, the Walk leads from sparsely settled hollows over mountain peaks with the only views being of deep woods and peak upon far peak of that special sharp blue color seen nowhere else. It is a short ride (three and a half hours) by good bus service from New York City, a swift transition from the most heavily populated region in the country to a remote mountain fastness. Here the mountains crowd together, scarcely leaving room for roads and tiny communities in the hollows and cloves (a Dutch word for steep-sided valleys).

Pine Hill

The area was opened up in the early 1800s for the vast hemlock forest whose bark was used in tanning. The forests, and hence the tanneries, lasted for 50 years. The hardwood forests that grew up in place of the vanquished hemlocks were and still are exploited for containers and furniture, but the area remains almost entirely wooded. The exceptions are small farms that you will find on unlikely ground, mostly deserted and starting to return to woodland. These farms were developed to support the horses and mules needed to harvest and transport the hemlock bark. Thus you will see ruined stone walls meandering up steep, now-wooded slopes, small clearings with an occasional stunted apple tree, or foundations of old farmhouses, pathetic remnants of past hopes and aspirations.

The Walk spans four mountain peaks, traverses sections of virgin forest, follows sparkling mountain streams and stops at night at interesting places. The way is well marked, the footing mostly good. The Walk is moderately challenging in spite of the short distances, because of the elevations gained.

We recommend that you start at Big Indian, that the second overnight be at the Appalachian Mountain Club (AMC) Mountain Gate Lodge, and that you avail yourselves of their bus service to be dropped off the third day at the southern trailhead to the Giant Ledges-Panther Trail, thus avoiding 4.3 miles of road walking and 1100 feet of climbing. If you come the other way, plan to stop at the Valley View Hotel 1.3 miles by road from the southern end of the Giant Ledge-Panther Trail, in order to make the first two day hikes more nearly equal in length.

OVERNIGHT POINTS

Pine Hill is a small, quiet community on a bypass of Rt 28. It is filled with old wooden houses reflecting early 20th-century architecture, preserved like flies caught in amber. All the houses have wide verandas across their fronts and sometimes along the sides. They have tall windows, with good-sized panes, often set in bays. The roofs are steeper than today and frequently have an A-shaped break in the front for the top bedroom windows. For all the similarity of architecture, there is a variety of size, siting and features that give that effect of diversity yet harmony not achieved in communities newly built today. A few of the Victorian edifices are so large that they must have been boarding houses. **Oliverea**, difficult to distinguish as a community, is three miles from Rt 28 on the Big Indian-Claryville road. This road parallels the upper reaches of the Esopus River in Big Indian Hollow, a valley just wide enough to carry a string of hardscrabble farms deep into the mountains. Oliverea must have been a market village for these farms. Unusual for the Catskill Park and especially for this relatively deserted section, there are some dozen active inns and lodges scattered along the road's eight-mile length. By the tiny Oliverea Post Office is a craft shop with the intriguing name of Puckihuddle Products. Just north is a small general store. The McKinley Hollow Road, leading to the trail for Pinehill, is south of the post office. **Big Indian** and **Shandaken** are scattered small communities, the first along the Big Indian-Claryville road, just off Rt 28, the second three miles east on Rt 28. They have lost their village character by spreading out along the road, and thus have been robbed of most of their individuality.

1. BIG INDIAN—PINE HILL
5.4 mi (8.7 km) / 1600 ft (488 m)
This easy hike permits you to travel to or from the trailhead the same day, even if you live a considerable distance away. It is a

modest leg stretcher, getting you in shape for more strenuous hikes ahead. You leave Big Indian by a logging road, go by an old woods road up the narrow ravine of Lost Clove to a shoulder of Belleayre Mountain and then drop down an unused firetower road to the old-fashioned village of Pine Hill. The route is through deciduous woods with glimpses of the nearby peaks through the trees.

The first part of the hike up the clove has the charm that routes which hug the side of a steep ravine always afford. If the trees are not in full leaf, you will be able to see quite clearly ahead the mountain you are climbing and behind the valley from which you have come. Even in summer you will get some glimpses of these sights. The way is well blazed and the footing good to excellent.

WEST—Walk up the Big Indian-Oliverea road, from its junction with Rt 28, to Lost Clove Rd. Go R here on the Lost Clove Trail (red blazes), and in 1.0 mi, near the ending of the paved road, take a trail R. This leads to a fairly new logging road that climbs up the N side of Lost Clove. The area has been selectively cut over, and there are good views through the trees of Balsam to the S and Panther and Giant Slide to the E. In about a mile you leave the logging road for an old woods road, a welcome relief from the mud and rocks of the newer road, and soon reach the blue-blazed trail to Pine Hill (3.1 mi).

Belleayre Lean-to, typical of shelters found here, is 0.1 mi L on this trail and worth a small digression at lunch-time as it is nicely sited facing the Clove. Otherwise, back at the junction, go R on the blue-blazed trail, an old access road to the Belleayre Mt firetower (0.6 mi to the L). The old road, now smoothed by time, goes by easy gradients down to a paved road just at the Pine Hill town dump (4.6 mi). Go past the dump through the woods, under an abandoned narrow-gauge railroad (it served the towns along Rt 28 before the auto age), to Pine Hill (5.4 mi).

EAST—Go W on Main St in Pine Hill to Bonnieville Ave and L one block to Mill St. Here a sign points L to Belleayre Mt and blue blazes appear. Follow Mill St until it ends at the village dump; continue ahead around a locked gate to an old access road leading to Belleayre firetower. Take this road up to its junction with the red-blazed Lost Clove Trail, which you follow down Lost Clove. You will hit a paved road at 3.5 mi. Follow it to the Big Indian-Oliverea road. Go L 0.5 mi to Rt 28.

2. PINE HILL—OLIVEREA
10.2 mi (16.5 km)/2935 ft (895 m)

This is a moderately strenuous walk over two of the Catskill Mountains, the shapely cone of Balsam and the great lump of Belleayre. While there are few views unless the leaves are off the trees, the trail is interesting in itself, with constant changes in gradient and in footing, from gentle woods roads to steep rocky paths.

We hiked this section in November after a light snowfall on the peaks. The normal differences between valley and mountain were accentuated as we climbed from the gold and red glow of autumn foliage over leafless snow-covered summits and back. There was enough snow to show tracks, and what usually seem to hikers to be deserted paths were revealed as well traveled, being covered by a network of deer, squirrel, chipmunk, rabbit, mouse and bird tracks. We were even able to trace out by tracks and blood on the snow a woodland tragedy, where a fox stalked and caught a squirrel. The way is well marked and the footing is good.

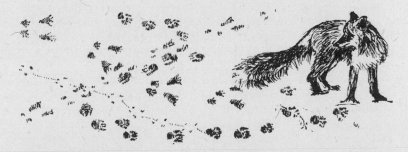

SOUTHEAST—Walk W on Main St in Pine Hill, and go L on Bonnieville Rd. You soon pass Mill St, where the blue-blazed trail from Big Indian comes in (you may have taken it yesterday). Continue up Bonnieville Rd to its end by the fenced-in town water settling tank (0.8 mi). Go L on a woods road and pick up blue markers (there is *no* trailhead sign here). In a short distance you reach an abandoned railroad, with the dam of the village reservoir

Balsam

beyond. Jog L on the railroad bed to a faint track (well marked) along the E side of the reservoir. This ends in a delightful old woods road that goes up the E side of Cathedral Glen through a stand of large hemlocks, giving way to small balsams that crowd the way and finally to hardwoods. The grade is easy here. At 1.8 mi you come to the bottom of Cathedral Glen Ski Trail. Now you have a rather dull 0.5 mi plod up the steep, wide ski trail (if there is snow, please keep to the edges of the trail—footprints are no fun to ski over). When you see a high board fence on the W side of the slope (2.3 mi), watch for a faint path on the E side of the trail (well marked but no sign). This leads steeply up through the woods and ends at a red-blazed trail (2.5 mi) which runs along the top of Belleayre Mt (3375 ft). Go L to the firetower (2.8 mi). If you think you have energy to spare before going to the firetower, go R on the red-blazed trail for 0.25 mi to Hirschland lean-to for a grand view back into Pine Hill.

Belleayre Mt is not a peak but a long, rather flat-topped ridge with few views. The firetower, at the E end of the ridge, stands astride the junction of three trails: the red-blazed one you were on, a blue-blazed one to Balsam Mt which you will take and another blue-blazed one going back to Pine Hill (which, if you came over to Pine Hill from Big Indian, you reached from the Lost Clove Trail, 0.6 mi below the firetower). A last word on the tower—it is closed to the public. However, everyone to whom we spoke had climbed it, and it does afford an unparalleled 360° view of the Catskills from the top.

From the tower go E on the blue-blazed trail signposted to Balsam Mt. It soon descends to a long saddle between Belleayre and Balsam. At 3.6 mi a yellow-blazed trail goes R down Mine Hollow to Rider lean-to. You continue on the blue-blazed trail, ascending Balsam at first gradually and then steeply over rocky ledges. Note the sudden change in trees as you go over the ledges—maples and beeches below giving way to yellow birches and evergreens above. This occurs everywhere in the Catskills at about 3000 ft elevation, but the demarcation line is much more marked here than anywhere else. The top of Balsam Mt (3620 ft, 4.6 mi) has a different ambience than Belleayre. It feels more like a mountaintop should, with widely spaced stunted trees and sedgy grass. As you move off the summit the trail passes over a relatively narrow ridge with one excellent viewpoint to the L, just off the trail, looking down into Big Indian, Lost Clove and the peaks to the E.

The trail now drops to the saddle between Balsam and Haynes mts and a junction at 5.5 mi with a red-blazed trail going between Oliverea and Mapledale. Go E (L) on this trail. It descends gradually at first but soon becomes a long, steep and very rocky descent into McKinley Hollow (this bit may be relocated to check erosion and to afford an easier gradient). At 6.8 mi the pitch eases off, and you pass two lean-tos. At 7.1 mi the trail reaches the McKinley Hollow auto road. The AMC Mountain Gate Lodge is just across the road. Oliverea and the Big Indian-Claryville road are a mile ahead. If you are staying at the Valley View Hotel, walk to Oliverea and go R (S) up the Big Indian-Claryville road for 2.1 mi.

NORTHWEST—From Oliverea walk W on McKinley Hollow Rd and in about 1.0 mi, opposite the AMC Mountain Gate Lodge, go L on a red-blazed trail. At 2.6 mi go R on a blue-blazed trail over Balsam Mt (3.5 mi) to Belleayre Mt firetower (5.3 mi). Take a red-blazed trail 0.2 mi to a blue-blazed trail R, and go down through Cathedral Glen to Pine Hill, 8.1 mi from Oliverea.

3. OLIVEREA—SHANDAKEN
11.1 mi (17.9 km)/2700 ft (820 m)
This is the most strenuous but most rewarding of the three days, as you have views all along the open rocks of the Giant Ledges and again from the summit of Panther Mountain. There is a good chance of seeing hawks and buzzards riding the air currents sweeping up the steep sides of the mountains here. Much of the forest is virgin timber—maple, beech and birch at the lower elevations and spruce and fir on the summits.

Judging from our hike in late April, it would be hard not to see deer on your way. Perhaps it was the season, but four times we came upon them. It is always a fresh thrill to look up and see before you these graceful creatures, petal ears pricked forward,

gentle shining eyes looking at you, body aquiver, with slender stick legs ready to bound away. Even one sighting enhances a hike, but four times makes a red-letter day.

The way is well marked, the footing poor to good.

NORTH—From the McKinley Hollow Rd in Oliverea, walk S uphill on the Big Indian-Claryville road. At 2.9 mi you pass the Valley View House Hotel on the R and 1.3 mi farther reach a parking lot R and the trailhead L. The mileages are from the trailhead. Go up a short steep grade on the yellow-blazed trail. It becomes a jeep road and levels off, going over smooth and rocky terrain through a hardwood forest—beech, maple and birch. The trail is apt to be muddy in spots here due to springs; split log bridges cross the muddiest places. During leafless months Giant Ledges and Panther Mt are visible through the trees to the L of the trail for the first 0.2 mi. Continue on the jeep road to the junction of the blue-blazed Giant Ledges-Panther Mt Trail (1.5 mi), and go L. The way narrows, gradually becomes steeper and more rocky and ends in a steep ascent to Giant Ledges' lean-to, 2.5 mi from Big Indian-Claryville road. You will get views S to Winnisook Lake and the Dennings area. A marked path leads L to a year-round, potable spring.

Pass in front of the lean-to and up a steep incline over boulders to Giant Ledges. Watch for the trail markers here since the way is not as visible as it was. Stunted trees struggle for footholds on the ledges, and lichens dot the trees and rocks. The trail soon levels off and provides spectacular views E of the Catskills and the Berkshires. For the next 0.5 mi the path parallels vertical ledges about 50 ft from the path. From these ledges you get excellent views of the Devil's Path Trail and Indian, Overlook and Plateau mts. You finally descend on sometimes steep rock ledges and through a hardwood forest to the saddle between Giant Ledges and Panther Mt. Note the large boulders strewn over the forest floor here, covered with lichens, mosses, ferns and small trees.

From the saddle the trail ascends somewhat steeply over rock shelves and boulders; in about 0.5 mi Slide and Wittenberg mts are visible R. The lookout marks the elevation (3500 ft) above which camping is forbidden because of the fragility of the environment. From the potable spring just above the lookout, descend steeply a short distance to a flat grassy area with a table-sized, smooth rock slab—a good stopping point to catch your breath and view the surrounding peaks. The trail stays level for about 1.5 mi at 3700 ft (indistinguishable summit at 3720 ft) as it winds through a forest of spruce and balsam. You then begin to descend along the NE side of Panther Mt via a succession of flat ridges to the top of Fox Hollow. Here there is a steep 1.0-mi section down through maples and oaks to the junction of the trail to Fox Hollow lean-to and spring (7.8 mi). Continue to follow the blue blazes down to Fox Hollow Rd, and go L for 2.5 mi to Rt 28. Shandaken is 0.5 mi L.

SOUTH—Walk E from Shandaken 0.5 mi on Rt 28 to the Fox Hollow Rd. Go R. The mileages from Shandaken are trailhead (blue-blazed) 3.0 mi; Panther Mt 7.4 mi; trail junction 10.3 mi. Go R on yellow-blazed trail 1.5 mi to Big Indian-Claryville road. Oliverea is R.

natural wall

PALISADES WALK
New York/New Jersey, 3 days, 26.9 miles (43.4 km)

SECTION	DISTANCE	OVERNIGHT POINTS
1	9.0 mi (14.5 km)	Alpine-Piermont
2	7.7 mi (12.4 km)	Piermont-Nyack
3	10.2 mi (16.5 km)	Nyack-Haverstraw

MAP—

Hikers Maps: No 24 Palisades (Sect 1), No 2 Blauvelt Park (Sects 1 & 2), No 8 Hook Mt Park (Sect 3). Order from Walking News, Inc, PO Box 352, New York, NY 10013.

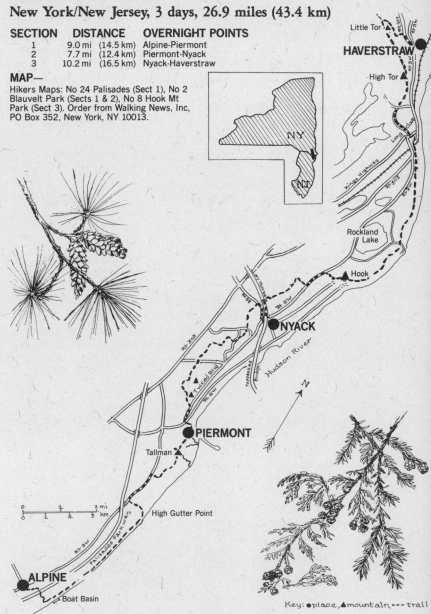

Key: ●place, ▲mountain, --- trail

TRANSPORTATION
Alpine and Haverstraw—bus (Mohawk Coach Lines, Inc)
                    NYC (freq serv)
All points—bus (Red and Tan Lines) NYC (freq serv)
Piermont—bus N to Nyack (Red and Tan Lines)

ACCOMMODATIONS (area code 214)
Nyack, NY 10960
    West Gate Motel, Rt 59 & Polhemus Rd   358-8100

Haverstraw, NY 10927
    Quality Motel, Rt 9W & Rt 202   429-4757

This is a remarkable hike along that unbelievably unspoiled stretch of land called the Palisades of the Hudson River. It starts at Alpine, only a few miles from the teaming millions of New York City, goes along the base of the Palisades' highest cliffs, climbs the escarpment and wanders by forest paths and woods roads to Nyack and Haverstraw. There is much to see—the old Dutch towns of Nyack and Haverstraw, the basaltic cone of High Tor to watch for ahead from miles away and finally to climb and gaze from back over the whole Walk. The Hudson River is always close at hand, sometimes at eye level and sometimes far below your feet.

The long ridge and cliffs of the Palisades are mostly the remains of a single volcanic diabase intrusion forces up through a rift eons ago. It often crystallized into the vertical columns, hexagonal or pentagonal in shape, seen so plainly on the cliff and quarry faces. Because it often erodes into what looks like steps, it is popularly known as trap rock, from the Swedish word *trapp* for stairs. The Palisades today are wooded and seemingly inaccessible yet were

Bombay Hook

once well peopled. In the southern section Dutch settlers prospered on tiny farms between the cliffs and the river, so many that "Under the Mountain" as it was called had nearly as many inhabitants as nearby Hackensack, the most heavily settled area in northern New Jersey. In the northern sections, farming settlements began at the sites of the present village of Piermont and the towns of Nyack and Haverstraw. The Dutch settled here in the 1680s. The region long retained its Dutchness, although settlers from other countries soon outnumbered the original ones. The early settlements were confined between the river and mountains until population pressure drove people through the gaps into the western valleys. In the northern sections farms were carved ever higher on the ridges, and today you will find stone walls running through the woods in seemingly inhospitable places.

While farming only temporarily removed the forests, the final threat to the Palisades was quarrying. The rock broke so readily into building stone and later into crushed stone for concrete and the area was so accessible to New York City by water transport that dozens of quarries began in operation over the whole length of the Palisades. By 1900 the destruction was so great that public opinion was aroused and the Palisades Interstate Park Commission was created. The commission and others, with the help of philanthropists like J D Rockefeller, gradually acquired land that is now the Palisades Interstate Park in New York and New Jersey and the five New York state parks along the river south of Haverstraw. You will pass an active quarry on the western slope of the Palisades at Long Clove and can see first-hand what the riverside cliffs were spared.

132

The two towns of Nyack and Haverstraw and the village of Pier-mont are places that time, in part, has passed by. Once bustling river ports for the hinterland of the Hackensack Valley, the coming of the railroad diminished their importance. The wave of surbur-ban development that engulfed the land west of the Palisades seems to have had little effect on these river habitations, and there is a serenity, especially in Piermont and Nyack, that more recently settled places lack. It is close to New York City and served by fre-quent bus service from there. The southern end is only 15 minutes from George Washington Bridge.

OVERNIGHT POINTS

Piermont is a quiet village located where the Spar Kill reaches the Hudson. Here a long finger of land juts out almost to the center of the Hudson, and south of this finger is a wide marsh. The village was once the terminus of a railroad that ran north along the river, forbidden by its charter to enter New Jersey. Thus Piermont was a transhipment point and drew its life from commerce. One of its amenities is the Clausland Bookstore, worth a browse while you wait for the bus. **Nyack** is a town that has stretched itself along the river and spilled west over a notch in the Palisades. The town center, a half-mile walk downhill from the West Gate Motel, is a charming blend of old houses and new shops, restaurants and a cinema. **Haverstraw** is on flat land by the river just where the Palisades turn inland. The town is overrun by industries and strip commercial at its north end, but retains its old flavor in the southern part. You will have to look for its charm.

1. ALPINE—PIERMONT
9.0 mi (14.5 km)/500 ft (150 m)
We hesitate to use the word *unique*, but this section is indeed one of a kind. It is close to populous New York yet seems so remote in its dramatic setting. Much of it is through a narrow wilderness wedged between the Hudson River and the magnificent 500-foot columnar cliffs of the lower Palisades. Just minutes from Manhat-

work goes on

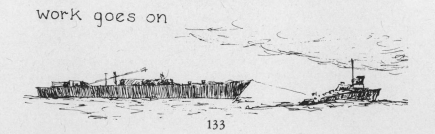

Sparkill

tan, we found it unpeopled on a weekday morning, deserted except for wheeling gulls, feeding ducks and a motley of songbirds.
The only man-made sounds to reach us were the distant chuffing
of tugs nosing barges along the river and the infrequent low
rumbling of trains on the far shore. The route leaves the bus at
Alpine on Rt 9W, drops down to the river and makes its way under
the towering cliffs by easy paths and intriguing slopes to the state
line. It ascends to a hemlock hollow and returns briefly to 9W
before wandering over the forest of Tallman Mountain Park to the
quiet river village of Piermont.

We have violated here an absolute rule of this book, the one
that there be lodgings at each overnight point. Piermont, alas,
lost its inns years ago. But the section is so choice and the buses
along Rt 9W so frequent that we have included it in the Walk.
Your last chore at the day's end is to take a bus north to the single
motel at Nyack. The bus, which goes down the main street of
Nyack, makes available to you a variety of interesting restaurants
and shops which you will not find in the vicinity of the motel
which lies up the hill from town center. The way is well marked,
the path highly visible and the footing poor (for a short distance
on a talus) to excellent.

NORTH—From the bus stop at Closter Dock Rd and Rt 9W, take
a tunnel E under the Palisades Pkwy to the blue-blazed Long Path
(LP). Go L (N) for about 0.5 mi and through another tunnel
under a road. Turn R downhill on an unblazed woods road that
takes you to the Shore Path just above the buildings of the Alpine
Boat Basin. If you want to visit the Basin go R. Your way is L (N),
and the path is blazed white with an occasional blue blaze ini-
tialed PHT. The trail here is an old carriage road, now mostly
grass, going past walls, stone stairs and old driveways of vanished
houses. The path starts out high above the river but soon comes

down and remains close to the water for several miles. In about 0.5 mi you pass Excelsior Dock, the first of several docks along the shore in this section. Ahead will be your first view of cliffs—Bombay Hook, a point that early sailing vessels found difficult to round with contrary winds. Before you reach the Hook, you pass a grassy expanse called Twombleys, believed to have been an Indian camp because of its pile of shells. At 1.3 mi from the Basin you pass under the cliffs of the Hook, highest in the Palisades. Here the shelf between the river and cliffs is wide, and there are fireplaces and plentiful driftwood if you want to cook lunch or just warm up (winter hikers note).

From the Hook N until you leave the shore the cliffs are always visible. At Ruckman Point, 0.5 mi N of the Hook, the cliffs drop a sheer 280 ft to the talus. You reach Forest View, a fairly wide area, partly wooded, 2.5 mi from the Basin. Some wag here had covered a "sacrificial" stone table with what we hoped was red paint. There are numerous white birches. Ahead you will get the best view of Indian Head, a striking silhouette on the vertical cliff edge. A trail goes L and ascends to the top of the Palisades escarpment to join the LP. It is signposted "Palisades Historical Trail" and is blazed light blue with the initials PHT; thus the mystery of those earlier blazes is solved. Continue N along the shore until a talus bars your way. You now have what seems like a mile of going up, down and around great boulders, but is perhaps less than 0.5 mi. It is a challenging but not a dangerous stretch and, taken slowly, should be a pleasure. There are many convenient stones on which to sit and watch the river traffic.

The last descent to a level path is called the Giant Stairs, 3.3 mi from the Basin. In another 0.5 mi the path passes a reedy place on the shore, the state line, where you begin a short steep ascent over slippery dirt to High Gutter Point, so named for a chute down which wood was pitched to fuel the river steamers. There is a trail going R (N) from the Shore Path at the top of the rise, but it does not go through. Go W on your white-blazed path a short distance until it ends at the LP coming downhill from the L (S) and turning

turkey buzzard

W. Now following blue blazes, go through the pleasant hemlock-clad Skunk Hollow, over a clear stream on an uncertain footbridge to a road going W a short distance down to Rt 9W at the entrance to the Lamont-Doherty Observatory. (An orange-blazed trail goes L shortly after the footbridge and reaches an old paved road that also goes R to Rt 9W at the Observatory.) Follow the blue blazes R (N) down Rt 9W a short distance to a woods road R that, alas, soon returns you to Rt 9W. After about 0.5 mi of road walking you pass Washington Spring St/Oak Tree Rd (traffic light here). Oak Tree Rd leads W 2.0 mi to the village of Tappan, now a historic site. E the road leads 1.0 mi to Sneden's Landing, once the western end of a ferry established in 1719. During the Revolution, Molly Sneden rowed the ferry across, thus the name.

Beyond Washington St 100 yds go R on a fine gravel road (closed to vehicles) into Tallman Mt Park. Opposite the ruins of a brick building the trail goes L on a level straight path. The building and low mounds of earth seen in the woods are the remains of an oil tank farm that once stood here. The path passes a little lake, crosses a paved road and reaches a small traffic circle in the park. Go W halfway around the circle to a faint path R (still blue blazed) which leads to the open woods and picnic area on top of Tallman Mt (really just a modest hump). There are good views here, E over the marshes of Piermont, with the meanders of Crum Kill and Spar Kill in view, and N over the village of Piermont. The trail drops to a gravel road going along the Spar Kill. You go L to an auto road running N into Piermont, pass the war memorial and cross the railroad tracks. The bus stops here, opposite the Clausland Bookstore.

SOUTH—Leave the bus stop in Piermont and walk S on Piermont Ave, following the blue blazes a short distance to a road bridge over Spar Kill. Just beyond the bridge go L on a gravel road to a path going R (S) up Tallman Mt. When you reach Lamont-Doherty Observatory (about 3.0 mi) go inside its entrance to a paved road going R (SE) off the main entrance road. The remaining distances from Piermont are Giant Stairs 4.5 mi; Forest View 5.5 mi; Alpine Boat Basin 8.0 mi; and Closter Dock Rd 9.0 mi.

2. PIERMONT—NYACK
7.7 mi (12.4 km)/500 ft (150 m)
The Palisades here is a hilly plateau caught between a residential strip along the river and the well populated towns of Tappan,

Orangeburg and Blauvelt. The trail climbs to and wanders over this plateau in a snake's dance that takes advantage of the most scenic areas. You will pass Rockland Cemetery, the resting place of "The Pathfinder" John C. Fremont, a fellow hiker who pioneered the West. For the troglodytes to assay, while the rest walk the ruins above, there is a long tunnel, part of a former rifle range. The way offers varied scenery—hemlock groves, pine plantations, oak woods, mountain streams and lookout points. It is not a strenuous walk and you can take your time, bird watching, flower hunting or just sitting on a rock, dreaming. The route is well marked, the footing good.

NORTH—Pick up the blue blazes of the LP in the center of Piermont, on Piermont Ave. Another trail, the Piermont, blazed yellow, parallels or shares the same trails as the LP on this section. Ignore the call of the yellow and stick to the blue, leading out of Piermont steeply uphill by village roads and a staircase to Rt 9W. Jog L to Highland Rd (the old Tweed Blvd) and go R on this road for 0.5 mi. Keep a sharp lookout for a faint track going L up through the woods (easier to find if you walk past it, miss seeing blazes and turn back, as we did). This path leads to Rockland Cemetery. There is also a grand view over the river. Follow the N edge of the cemetery for 100 yds to a path going W. You will climb gently from here along the S edge of the plateau with occasional glimpses L of Tappan and its suburbs. The path finally leaves the plateau edge, strikes generally NW and gradually descends through mostly deciduous forests to the paved Clausland Mt Rd, 2.8 mi from Piermont. Cross to a small parking lot and go by a woods road past a small pond. The path soon crosses a clear stream and then moves from path to woods road and back several times in a confusing manner. Don't hasten and you'll be able to unravel the way. In one or two places the blazes are quite far apart, adding to the problem.

You will come in a short time to a pine plantation of good-sized trees. Beyond is the remains of a rifle range. A concrete wall to the

R was the target area. A 3000-ft safety tunnel, an earth-topped dike, runs at right angles to this wall from its N end. The tunnel can be entered by a manhole at its W end and by a door at its E end and has frequent vents for light and air. It will add to your hiking experience, if you can tolerate confined spaces. Beyond the rifle range the trail follows a generally NE direction along various paths and through a hemlock grove to the paved Tweed Blvd. Go L uphill on the boulevard to the crest of the ridge. Here, at 4.8 mi there is a rocky viewpoint R, once the site of Balance Rock, destroyed by vandals in 1966. You can see both the Hudson and Hackensack valleys. Continue downhill on the boulevard for about 0.3 mi to a gravel road R, leading you through the grounds of Nyack Missionary College to Bradley Hill Rd. Jog L to a path going over a wooded knoll to a paved road which runs down to Rt 59. Leave the blazes here and go R (E) on Rt 59, passing under the NY Thruway. Just beyond, to the L, is the West Gate Motel. The center of Nyack with restaurants, movie and stores is 0.5 mi farther on.

SOUTH—Go W on Rt 59 from the West Gate Motel to the first traffic light. Go L on Waldron Ave and pick up the blue blazes of the LP. In 100 yds take a R fork to Towt Rd; then go L uphill past two houses and enter the woods on a path along a stone wall. Follow the path over a wooded knoll, with views of the Hudson Valley and Nyack below, to a paved road. Jog L to Nyack Missionary College and go through its grounds to a gravel road leading to Tweed Blvd. Follow NORTH directions in reverse from here. Mileages are Tweed Blvd 2.9 mi; Clausland Mt Rd. 4.9 mi. When you reach Rt 9W jog L to a road going downhill into Piermont.

3. NYACK—HAVERSTRAW
10.2 mi (16.5 km)/800 ft (240 m)

This is a high ridge hike. You go over the long Hook Mountain, which makes a great curve from Nyack to the notch at Long Clove; around a vast quarry to Short Clove; and finally by the ridge and cones of High Tor and Little Tor, with their panoramic views. There is a strong sense of being above it all, partly because of the elevation, partly the isolation and partly the far away views of habitation, with the towns on the distant shore of the Hudson to the east and the far-removed heavily populated areas to the west.

A life-long resident told us of a youthful indiscretion on High Tor while camping out one wet autumn weekend. He put his boots near the fire to dry, went to sleep and awakened in the morning to nothing but the charred soles and metal eyelets lying on fresh-fallen snow. With Yankee ingenuity he sacrificed a blanket for a pair of makeshift boots and hobbled down the mountain, sadder but wiser. It still amused him to speculate on what anyone following his strange tracks in the snow would have made of them.

NORTH—Walk N from the West Gate Motel on Rt 59 to Mountainview Rd and pick up the blue blazes of the LP. Go R (N) a short distance to a path going R through woods. This leads up to and around an apartment complex and down through woods to Christian Herald Rd; go R to its intersection with Rt 9W. Go L (N) on Rt 9W for about 300 yds to a path R into the woods. This goes to a short length of the Tweed Blvd, so named because local politicians attempted unsuccessfully to emulate Boss Tweed and his New York boulevards.

Go N on the boulevard, now littered by large fallen rocks, to a path leading up the S slope of Hook Mt to its summit (729 ft, 2.0 mi). The top commands a complete circular view—ahead to High Tor, W to the Ramapos, S to Piermont and E to the Hudson River. Thus most of two days' walks is visible. The long ridge of Hook Mt stretches another 5.0 mi ahead. The path now goes down and up, by an old quarry, and meets the old boulevard again. The footing here is delightful, but all too soon you must go down a steep and slippery dirt slope to the paved Rockland Landing Rd (3.6 mi). This leads L to Rockland Lake, now a park but once the site of a great ice-harvesting industry, from 1831 to 1924. The superiority of the ice from its spring-fed waters was widely recognized. At one time 4000 men worked to cut the ice, place it in sawdust-packed icehouses and, when needed, bring it over to Rockland Landing for carrying by boat to New York City.

Cross the road, go uphill past a small cemetery and along a ridge and drop down to Trough Hollow, once the main road from Rockland Lake village to the river and the site of a cog railway used to carry the ice. There is now only a small wire enclosure serving some obscure purpose. Beyond the hollow the trail goes along a stone wall above the parking lot of the park golf course. There is a short trail down to the N end of this lot where there is a refreshment stand, open in the summer only. Continuing on your way, you have a long uneventful stroll over wooded knolls, with an occasional view. We saw our first Dutchman's-breeches here in mid-April; they really do look like hosts of tiny cream-colored pantaloons hung upside down to dry on the feathery green foliage. In places they covered the hillside. At 6.0 mi you drop down to Long Clove, a notch in the ridge, cross Rt 9W to a paved road opposite that goes W around a huge quarry to a road through Short Clove. Go R uphill on this paved road 200 yds to a path L (N). This takes you by an easy grade to the two steps up High Tor, steep, rocky pitches on which you may need a hand or two. You will pass the white-blazed Deer Path that leads R (E) down to Rt 9W about 0.5 mi S of the old Haverstraw RR station (sorry, no passenger trains anymore). Finally reaching High Tor (827 ft), the highest point on the Palisades, you will have the magnificent views you have so well earned. Haverstraw is at your feet, and the river spreads out N and S. Behind you stretches the ridge in a great arc back to Nyack. The peninsula off Piermont is visible, and on a clear day New York's high buildings will loom over the farthest ridges. The ridges of the Ramapos and the succeeding ridges of the Appalachian chain can be seen W. Sit awhile and contemplate this large chunk of nature. You will regretfully leave it.

Your path off High Tor, much easier than the route up, goes W down to a woods road running N. A mile or so beyond, there is a clear crossroad with a wide path running R 0.3 mi to Little Tor. You continue straight ahead, and in 0.5 mi the white-blazed Little Tor Trail goes sharply R (not signposted). Take it down to Dowd St in Haverstraw. Follow Dowd St to W Side Ave (Rt 202); the Quality Motel is a short distance to the R (E).

SOUTH—Walk W on Rt 202 from its intersection with RT 9W. Turn L on Dowd St, a short street leading to an apartment house. Just where it turns sharply L to reach the buildings, go straight ahead (W) into the woods and pick up a white-blazed trail slanting uphill. It ends at the LP in about 1.0 mi. Go L (S). The mileages are High Tor 2.3 mi; Long Clove 4.2 mi; Rockland Landing Rd 6.6 mi; Hook Mt 8.2 mi.

from High Tor

WAWAYANDA WALK
New Jersey/New York, 3 days, 30.9 miles (49.8 km)

SECTION	DISTANCE		OVERNIGHT POINTS
1	7.3 mi	(11.8 km)	Rt 94 (Maple Grange)-Warwick Turnpike
2	9.8 mi	(15.8 km)	Warwick Turnpike-Greenwood Lake Village
3	13.8 mi	(22.3 km)	Greenwood Lake Village-Rt 17
1a	5.0 mi	(8.1 km)	Rt 511 (S Greenwood Lake)-Lakeside
2a	6.2 mi	(10.0 km)	Lakeside-Greenwood Lake Village

MAP—

Hikers Maps: No 21B Greenwood Lake S (Sects 1, 2, 1a, 2a), No 21A Greenwood Lake N (Sect 3). Order from Walking News, Inc, PO Box 352, New York, NY 10013.

142

TRANSPORTATION
Rt 94—Taxi, Warwick (8.0 mi); bus (Warwick Stage), Warwick-
NYC freq serv)
Warwick Turnpike—bus (Warwick Stage), Warwick-NYC
1 r/t daily weekdays
Greenwood Lake Village—bus (Warwick Stage), NYC (freq serv)
Lakeside, S Greenwood Lake—bus (Warwick Stage), NYC
(freq serv)
Mt Peter—bus (Warwick Stage), NYC (freq serv)
Rt 17—bus (Short Line), NYC (stops on signal, freq serv)

ACCOMMODATIONS (area codes 201 & 914)
Rt 94, Vernon, NJ 07462
    Appalachian Motel   201-288-4242

Warwick Turnpike,Warwick NY 10990
    Willowbrook Inn, PO Box 375   201-853-7728

Greenwood Lake, NY 10925
    Breezy Point Inn   914-477-8100
    Motel Cafe du Lac, Lakeside   477-8826
    New Continental Hotel, Lakeside   477-2456

Rt 17, Tuxedo Park, NY 10987
    Red Apple Motel   351-4747

This is a modestly strenuous hike on the Appalachian Trail that crisscrosses the New Jersey/New York state line. Taken from west to east, which we recommend, it grows progressively more strenuous, the third day going over four separate mountain peaks. The way is almost entirely on woods roads and paths, through deciduous forests generally but also through handsome groves of hemlocks,

some with good-sized trees. There are frequent treeless high points, with nearly four continuous miles of open ridge walking the middle day. En route you stay one night at an old boarding house serving family-style meals, and the other night you have a choice of several comfortable inns situated on the shores of Greenwood Lake. The way is well marked and the trail well maintained. Access to the Walk is less than two hours from New York City by frequent bus service, which reaches all the overnight and end points, except Rt 94, for maximum flexibility in trip planning. For Rt 94 you will have to take a taxi from Warwick eight miles. Because of that long taxi ride and because the Willowbrook Inn may not always be open, we give a very easy two-day or a moderate one-day option to sections 1 and 2 (directions given NORTH only).

A visit to the library of Greenwood Lake Village turned up a wealth of local historical material all collected by the Village Historian. We found that the area was first inhabited by Leni Lenape Indians who were little disturbed by the Dutch arrival in 1609. A century later the Indians granted land to English settlers through a patent bearing the intriguing name of Cheesecock's. The area was early noted for its iron industry. Greenwood Lake was first dammed in 1768 to provide water to power the furnaces and forges. To us the most interesting product from this industry was the great chain which was laid across the Hudson River at West Point during the Revolution to block British ships from ascending the river. The forges were kept working day and night for six weeks, and as fast as the iron links were forged, they were transported to West Point by local farmers in their wagons. Each link weighed 500 pounds and there were 700 links to move, no mean feat of forging and moving.

OVERNIGHT POINTS

Willowbrook Inn is an old frame hotel that has catered for years to hikers on the Appalachian Trail. It has family-style meals and the vast painting on the dining room wall is remarkable. **Greenwood Lake Village** lies at the north end of Greenwood Lake. The lake not only supported the early iron industry but also provided water for the Morris-Essex Canal from the 1830s. Later, its clear waters were sold to New York City in the form of ice, one icehouse alone holding 90,000 frozen tons. Willy Ley shot off a mail rocket from the frozen lake surface in 1933; although he delivered the mail from one state to another (the New York/New Jersey state line cuts the lake in half) and stamps were printed for the occasion, the length of the rocket flight (300 yards) could hardly be called a success. How far rockets have come! The major change to the life around the lake came with the building of a railroad to the water's lower end in 1875. New York City people could reach the lake in two hours, a time hardly bettered by the auto. Hotels and boarding houses sprang up, and three steamboats were launched to distribute the visitors around the lake. Some idea of the volume of visitors can be gained from the fact that two boats could carry 100 passengers each and the third 400! The auto changed all this however, and Greenwood Lake suffered the neglect which befell so many other beautiful areas near New York that bloomed and faded with the railroads. Its charms were rediscovered in the 1930s by vaudeville and theatrical people, and many of the cottages around the lake belong to them or their children.

1. RT 94 (MAPLE GRANGE)—WARWICK TURNPIKE
7.3 mi (11.8 km)/996 ft (304 m)
This is a moderate beginning to a grand three-day walk across high forested land. Though short, the trail changes elevation frequently enough that trail's end will be reached none too soon. Going east, the trail climbs steeply nearly 1000 feet out of the Ver-

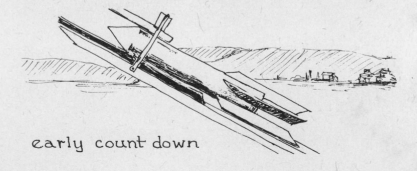

early count down

non Valley to Wawayanda Mountain, from which there are magnificent views. After following the mountain edge for nearly a mile, the trail wanders through hemlock and deciduous forests. It crosses old stone walls, reminding you that much of the now heavily forested land was once laboriously cleared for agriculture and grazing. The character of the trail is constantly changing so that you never grow weary from sameness—steep rocky pitches, soft leafy mold, boggy ground, and firm old woods roads. There are frequent glimpses (less in summer) of the farmlands of the Vernon and Warwick valleys and of distant wooded ranges. The way is generally well blazed, the footing good.

We hiked this route in early March, and snow and ice still clung to north slopes and hollows. At one point we emerged from a particularly dark, cold and snowy hemlock grove into open sunny land. The snow cover stopped abruptly as if at an invisible boundary, just as it does in C. S. Lewis' children's classic "The Lion, the Witch and the Wardrobe." So, feeling that we were stepping out of the White Witch's domain, we had to turn back and jeer at that icy queen.

EAST—The trail leaves Rt 94 midway between Warwick, NY, and Hamburg, NJ, just where the Maple Grange Rd (Sussex Rt 515) comes in (8.0 mi S of Warwick, 1.7 mi N of Vernon, NJ). There is a large metal Appalachian Trail (AT) sign opposite the intersection. The trail goes SE across farmland, with white blazes on the trees along the field edge. In about 0.2 mi you jog L, enter a cutover deciduous forest and start climbing steeply on logging roads and footpaths up the NW slope of Wawayanda Mt (named by the Leni-Lenape Indians and meaning "water on the mountain"). As the way becomes rockier, you leave the lumbered area and climb

domain of the White Witch

through hemlock, somber and cool at any season. As the slope grows less steep, the trail swings NE and comes out of the hemlocks onto the rocky edge of the mountain, backed by a sparse deciduous forest (1.1 mi). From here the trail runs for about 0.7 mi along this edge, giving frequent views of the Vernon Valley and the opposite Pochuk Mt. Soon you go E across the broken top of the mountain, frequently crossing stone walls and old roads, evidence of early settlers. Yellow blazes join the white, but just ignore them. The trail moves down the side of a stream in hemlocks and climbs over two knobs to cross the Barrett Rd at a large pine (3.8 mi). Cross the road into the forest opposite, and go downhill to an old woods road at the edge of a field—views N of Adam and Eve mts and the distant Shawangunks (pronounced *shon-gum*). Go R (E) on this road for about 0.2 mi to fainter road R (we missed the double blazes here and ended 200 yds beyond by the cellar of an old farmstead—a lesson to us to watch the blazes). Follow this fainter road for less than a mile to a meadow, with one 300-yd detour into the woods to avoid a boggy stretch. Cross the meadow in the direction you entered (no blazes here) to the woods road beyond, and very shortly you will reach the old Iron Mt Rd. Go L, cross an old wood-floored iron bridge and continue straight ahead up a hill past an abandoned white farmhouse (you can see the house from the bridge or just beyond). At 5.5 mi the trail goes R into the woods (well marked here) for 0.5 mi and crosses a knob to the unpaved Wawayanda Rd. Go R for about 0.3 mi and L back into the woods, cross a swampy area (small bridges and planks help), go over a small ridge and down the edge of a field to the paved Warwick Tpk (6.6 mi). The Willowbrook Inn is L (N) downhill 0.7 mi.

WEST—Walk S on the Warwick Tpk from the Willowbrook Inn for 0.7 mi. Shortly after you pass the Maplebrook Farm, you will come to a field on your R. The trail goes R uphill along the far (S) edge of this field, with the first white blaze in the upper corner of the field. Follow this trail to a dirt road and jog R for 0.2 mi; reenter the woods L for 0.5 mi to the dirt Iron Mt Rd (1.8 mi). Go L on this road to an iron bridge, cross and take a trail R to Barrett Rd (3.5 mi). (Just before Barrett Rd there is a short section leading L off the woods road that is easy to miss. You may therefore reach Barrett Rd while still on the woods road, about 0.2 mi N of the trail crossing. If so, go L uphill. The trail R is marked by a large pine tree.) From Barrett Rd you go over Wawayanda Mt to its W edge. The trail parallels the ledges here in open woods, enters a hemlock grove and turns W downhill by the first stream. Go steeply down through a partly cut-over forest and cross a wide meadow to Rt 94.

2. WARWICK TURNPIKE— GREENWOOD LAKE VILLAGE

9.8 mi (15.8 km), 810 ft (247 m)

Nearly half this hike is along the level rocky spine of the mountains bordering the west shore of Greenwood Lake, with magnificent views to the east of the Greenwood Lake valley, the Ramapo hills and, on a clear day, the New York skyline. It is the longest walk continually above the trees that we have found in the Mid-Atlantic states. There is an escape route off the crest if the weather turns severe, and there is considerable protection by the trees, so the exposed section is quite safe. The remainder of the hike is through deciduous and evergreen forests, with constantly changing footing. The way is well marked and the footing good to excellent.

EAST—Walk S from the Willowbrook Inn on the Warwick Tpk. Go about 0.2 mi past the Maplebrook Farm to a double blaze on a big tree on the L (E) side of the road (0.7 mi). On this trail go through a scrubby deciduous woods with a small swamp to negotiate, tussock by tussock, then through an open field with good views N. At the far (E) edge of the field you enter woods again and drop down to an old woods road. Go L keeping watch for a double blaze to take you R off the road (we found ourselves following painted-out blazes here as the AT once went N of this track). At 2.8 mi you reach the paved Brady Rd; go L (N) and soon re-enter the woods. In a short distance you will pass on your L a rust-colored pile of stones, on the other side of which is the cut of the old Centennial iron mine, one of the many in the region. At 3.3 mi you reach Long House Creek, the outlet of Upper Greenwood Lake. In March 1981 the footbridge, built in 1976, had fallen; a jury-rig of logs and the remains of the bridge led us precariously across (the nearby woods are full of balance poles). On the E side of the stream go L (N) on an unpaved road past a few small houses and then R (E) on a forest path leading over a series of small ridges to the top ridge of Bearfort Mt (4.3 mi). After leaving the road, you will pass the shell of an old car. We wondered at the misplaced ingenuity and labor that got it there.

Your magnificent views start when you reach the crest of the mountain. Just below you is the small Surprise Lake, in the

148

distance are the Ramapo hills and at the edge of the sky you may see New York City. Greenwood Lake is still hidden by the bulk of the mountain. The trail now runs N along Bearfort and then Bellvale mts. with little change in elevation. Most of the way is on rocky spines, as if you were moving along the back of some vast dinosaur. At 4.8 mi a blue-blazed trail goes R (E) leading to the State Line Trail and the Bearfort Ridge Trail.

At 5.3 mi you reach Prospect Rock, 1433 ft, with full views N, E and S. The lower end of Greenwood Lake (appears to the SE and Dutch Hollow to the NE. Please sign the register here, as it helps those who maintain the trail prove trail usage. At 6.3 mi you cross Furnace Brook, a welcome crystal stream. You soon come to a clearing surrounded by large hemlocks. Ignore the scattered blue blazes, cross the clearing and pick up the white blazes on the other side. At 8.0 mi the unmarked Mother Rialto Trail goes L (W), and finally, at 8.8 mi, the blue-on-white blazed Mountain Spring Trail goes R (E) 0.7 mi down to Greenwood Lake Village. The trail intersection is an unmistakable fork, as this side trail was once a woods road. A steep 600-ft drop to the lakeshore, the trail reaches Rt 210 just opposite the Cove Marina. Breezy Point Inn is 0.3 mi R (S), and the bus stop in the center of the village is 0.4 mi L (N). WEST—The trailhead at Greenwood Lake Village, blazed blue on white but badly faded (1981), is a grassy woods road going W uphill from Rt 210 just S of a gas station and opposite the Cove Marina, 0.5 mi S of the center of the village. Just N of the trailhead is a converted bowling alley, a large building with the unmistakable curved roof. (Once found, the trailhead is obvious,

teeter over

but an early reconnaissance trip failed to find it, and no local people we talked to had ever heard of it; so we have made our directions more explicit than usual.) Go steeply uphill for 0.7 mi (watch for an unmarked fork L) to the AT (white blazed), and go L (S) along Bellvale and Bearfort mts. You will pass successively (in miles from the Breezy Point Inn) Furnace Brook (3.5 mi); Prospect Rock (4.5 mi); Long House Creek (6.5 mi); Brady Rd (7.0 mi); Warwick Tpk (9.2 mi). The Willowbrook Inn is 0.7 mi R (N) on the turnpike.

Bearfort Ridge

3. GREENWOOD LAKE VILLAGE—RT 17
13.8 mi (22.3 km)/2200 ft (671 m)

This is the most strenuous section of the Walk but well worth the extra effort. The way is constantly changing in scenery and footing. You climb four peaks, scramble on ledges, pass a handsome waterfall and skirt an unspoiled mountain lake. It is the wildest of the sections even though it crosses four roads. It contains the famous Agony Grind, a 600-foot dramatic pitch above Rt 17. The way is well marked, the footing good to excellent. If you would like to shorten the trip a bit, 2.4 miles (and a 600-ft climb, when heading E) can be avoided by busing between Greenwood Lake Village and Mt Peter.

EAST—The trailhead is 0.5 mi S of the center of Greenwood Lake Village on Rt 210 (see Section 2). Retrace your steps 0.7 mi to the AT, blazed white. Go R (N), with little change of elevation, to Rt 17a and the top of Mt Peter (1130 ft, 2.4 mi from Rt 210). Jog R (E) 100 yds to an easy woods road that leads gently downhill for about a mile to a path R (E). In a short distance you scramble up the Eastern Pinnacles, a small spine of conglomerate rock 15-20 ft high (4.1 mi). Here there are good views N, E and S over the Greenwood Lake Valley. Farther on is Cat Rock, a similar outcropping, with views W (a faint unmarked path goes 100 yds along the E flank of Cat Rock if you want to avoid the somewhat narrow top). In 0.5 mi a blue-blazed trail leads L 100 yds to a spring.

From Cat Rock you pass a level area used for campsites and then travel on a woods road for about a mile through a sparse deciduous forest over what once was farmland. Turn R (E) downhill on a new path (1981) to the paved Lakes Rd at 6.0 mi. Cross the road down to a footbridge over Trout Brook. The trail wanders up the banks of the brook through a dense hemlock grove. At 6.2 mi you climb a cleft by Fitzgerald Falls, a 25-ft drop of the brook over mossy rocks. At 7.0 mi a green-on-white blazed trail goes L (N), making a loop which rejoins the AT in about a mile. Stay with the white blazes. At 7.4 mi the blue-blazed Allis Trail goes R (2.0 mi to Rt 17a). From the large rock at this junction you can see the Delaware Water Gap and High Point monument to the W and Bellvale Mt to the SW. You continue on the AT over fairly level country to E Mombasha High Point (1280 ft, 8.1 mi) and pass the returning green-white blazed loop trail on L (W). You will have good views from this summit, including Schunemunk Mt to the NE and Mombasha Lake below.

The trail now descends, steeply at first, to the paved W Mombasha Rd just at the S end of Mombasha Lake (9.0 mi). Go R (S) on the road to a low stile and L (E) into a field. Go along the field edge into woods, along the shore of a small lake and over a knoll. You come to a 100-ft cliff up which you must scramble (formidable only at a distance) to a lovely ledge walk on the top of Buchanan Mt (9.8 mi). The tips of great hemlocks which grow from the valley below reach eye-level here. Watch for a bronze memorial tablet to Peter Buck, who maintained this section at one time. He died, the way many hikers would like to, while hiking on the trail. From the ledges you descend to a small valley and climb again to a second summit before descending to E Mombasha Rd (10.8 mi). Cross to a woods road which shortly brings you to a good footbridge over the inlet to beautiful Little Dam Lake. The trail skirts the edge of the lake for 0.7 mi and then climbs over a hemlock-clad ridge to the paved Old Orange Tpk (12.0 mi). (You may hear firing from a nearby rifle range.) Jog L on the road to a trail going R (NE), and climb steeply along and over rocky ledges to a rocky tableland. At 12.3 mi you reach a knoll from which you can see in all directions, even N to the Catskill Mts. At 12.9 mi you reach the summit of Arden Mt (1130 ft) with views W to Mombasha Lake, Mombasha High Point and Bellvale Mt. Please sign the trail register here. Beyond the summit you can look down into the Ramapo Valley and the tiny cars crawling along the Thruway and Rt 17. Soon you begin the Agony Grind, dropping 600 ft in about 0.2 mi to Rt 17. On Rt 17 you can flag the Short Line buses to New York City or walk 2.5 mi S to the Red Apple Motel and Tuxedo Inn.

WEST—Go 2.5 mi N of the Red Apple Motel in Southfields to the signposted AT which crosses Rt 17 just by a parking area and telephone kiosk on the E side of the road. Go W steeply uphill to the rocky tableland of Arden Mt. The way is straight-forward to Mt Peter (see EAST description). The mileages are Old Orange Tpk 1.8 mi; E Mombasha Rd 3.0 mi; Buchanan Mt 4.0 mi; W Mombasha Rd 4.8 mi; Mombasha High Point 5.7 mi; Lakes Rd 7.8 mi; Eastern Pinnacles 9.7 mi; Mt Peter 11.1 mi. At Mt Peter, go R (W) for 100 yds on Rt 17a to a path going S. At 12.8 mi you reach the blue-on-white blazed Mountain Spring Trail. Go L (E) to Greenwood Lake.

Greenwood Lake

1a. SOUTH GREENWOOD LAKE—LAKESIDE
5.0 mi (8.1 km)/600 ft (183 m)

NORTH—From the S end of Greenwood Lake walk W on the Warwick Tpk for 0.5 mi and turn R (N) on a rocky woods road, marked by three square white blazes on a rock (Bearfort Ridge Trail). In 100 yds you turn L and wind uphill, sometimes steeply, to the top of Bearfort Mt. You then follow a series of bare rock ridges N, with marvelous views of Greenwood and Upper Greenwood lakes and the mountains beyond, with New York City on the SE skyline. At 3.0 mi the trail ends at the Walther Trail, blazed yellow. Go R on this trail, past Surprise Lake (nice picnic spot by the lake), to its end at State Line Trail, blazed blue-on-white (4.0

mi). Go R (E) downhill to Rt 511/210 just S of the NY/NJ state line (5.0 mi). Motel Cafe du Lac is 0.1 mi L (N) and the New Continental Hotel is 1.3 mi L (N).

mountain laurel

2a. LAKESIDE—GREENWOOD LAKE VILLAGE
6.2 mi (10.0 km)/700 ft (210 m)
NORTH—Take the State Line Trail from Rt 511/210 just S of the NY/NJ state line, opposite the Greenwood Lake Marina. A gravel road, with a chain across, goes uphill a few yds to a parking lot. The trail goes L from this lot, blazed blue-on-white (blazes are sparse at first). In 1.2 mi you reach the AT, blazed white, passing the Walther Trail (yellow blazes) on the way. Go R (N) on the AT and follow the EAST directions of Section 2.
Note: To combine 1a and 2a into one day's hike, follow the directions for 1a until you reach the State Line Trail. Go L instead of R on this trail, and you will soon reach the AT, blazed white. Go R on the AT and follow the EAST directions of Section 2. The total distance is 9.2 mi.

DELAWARE CANAL WALK
Pennsylvania, 4 days, 45.9 miles (74.0 km)

SECTION	DISTANCE		OVERNIGHT POINTS
1	11.5 mi	(18.5 km)	Yardley-New Hope
2	13.1 mi	(21.1 km)	New Hope-Golden Pheasant Inn
3	13.1 mi	(21.1 km)	Golden Pheasant Inn-Riegelsville
4	8.2 mi	(13.2 km)	Riegelsville-Easton

MAP—
No map needed.

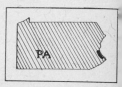

PA

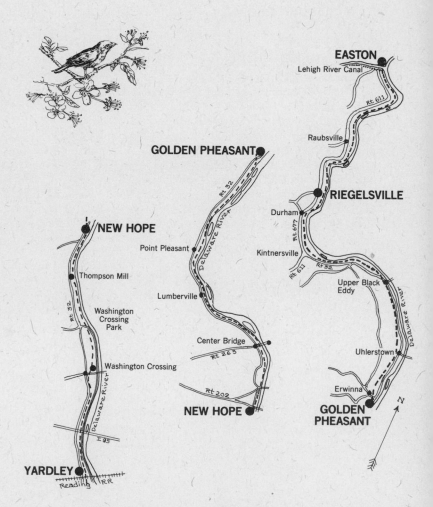

TRANSPORTATION
Yardley—train (SEPTA Reading), Phila (freq serv)
Easton—bus (Trailways) Phila, 4 r/t dly
            (Transport of NJ) New York/Harrisburg (freq serv)

ACCOMMODATIONS (area code 215)
Washington Crossing, PA 18977
    Washington Crossing Inn   493-3634

New Hope, PA 18938
    Allison's   862-5237
    Logan Inn   862-5134
    Pam Minford's Hacienda   862-2078
    The Inn at Phillips Mill   862-9919

Centre Bridge, PA 18938*
    Centre Bridge Inn   862-2048

Lumberville, PA 18933*
    Black Bass Hotel   297-5770
    1740 House   297-5661

Point Pleasant, PA 18950*
    Innisfree   297-8329

Erwinna, PA 18920
    Golden Pheasant Inn   294-9595

Upper Black Eddy, PA 18972
    Upper Black Eddy Hotel   982-5554
    Jason House   982-5457

Riegelsville, PA 18077
    Riegelsville Hotel   749-2092

Easton, PA 18042
    Hotel Easton   253-6181
    Sheraton Hotel   253-9131

*See Section 2, New Hope-Golden Pheasant, for locations.

A stroll into history, this Walk along the towpath of the Delaware Canal introduces you to canal life. Opened in 1832 and operated for just under 100 years, the canal ran from Easton, where it met the canal along the Lehigh River, down to tidewater at Bristol. Most of its length is now restored and incorporated as the Roosevelt State Park. The Walk covers most of the canal's original 60-mile length.

To the walker the principal interests are the features of the canal itself—locks, bridges, aqueducts and overflows; the villages that sprang up to serve the waterway, not too much changed from canal days; and the handsome countryside, still rural, that lies along the Delaware River.

The overnight points have charming country inns in which to stay, and New Hope is noted for its shops and theater. There is the Canal Museum at Easton, well worth several hours' visit. Both ends of the Walk have good transportation to Philadelphia, and Easton is reached by frequent bus service from New York.

The footing is excellent—level and grassy—and we challenge anyone to get lost on the way. The route can also be done by canoe or bicycle, but you will see more on foot. We hesitate to mention that there are numerous good restaurants along the route, obviating the trail lunch but hard on the waistline and pocketbook. The Walk can be done at any time of the year, each season bringing its own charm. Three sections have inns at intermediate points and could, if desired, be broken into a more than one-day hike, allowing either more leisure or more exploration.

OVERNIGHT POINTS

Yardley, now on the northern edge of a residential belt extending along the Delaware River from Morrisville, once was a hamlet called Yardleyville after its first settler William Yardley, who came in 1682. His son operated a ferry here from 1722. The Walk takes you past several fine old residences before you reach the canal.
New Hope is a small town that grew from a ferry crossing licensed in 1722. Although the river is crossed now by a relatively modern auto bridge, the memory of the old way is kept alive in the name of Ferry Street and in the Logan Inn, part of which is the old tavern built in 1727 to serve the ferry traffic. Coming upon the town's Main Street after walking along the quiet canal towpath, you will find, especially on a weekend, the way lined with people and shops.

The community had flourished in colonial times because of its location by the water power of the river and local tributaries. This original prosperity was enhanced by the building of the canal, but by the end of the 19th century the town had faded into obscurity. In the early part of this century artists and crafts people settled here for its quiet charm and pastoral beauty, and the patrons came to them, leading to the touristy atmosphere which prevails today. However, it takes only a few moments stroll away from Main Street to regain the feeling of old-time charm. This is not surprising when you realize that of the 210 buildings that were there in 1876, 181 are still standing today. Most shops carry the walking tour guide put out by the local historical society, a great help in seeing New Hope. For entertainment there is the Bucks County Playhouse housed in a converted old mill (May-Nov). The New Hope-Ivyland Railroad operates steam train excursions in the summer, and the New Hope Mule Barge has one-hour excursion rides or longer charter rides year-round. **Golden Pheasant Inn** stands alone between the towpath and the river road, a stone's throw from the river. This was once a tavern run by Jacob Oberacker. Here the canalmen could stop for refreshment, perhaps beer and salt cakes (much like thick pretzels.) **Riegelsville** is a quiet river village by an old suspension bridge which replaced a wooden covered bridge destroyed in the disastrous flood of 1903. There are a number of interesting buildings to see—the Riegelsville Hotel (1828), some old red brick houses next door and a church and large residences along the river road. The city of **Easton** stands at the confluence of the Delaware and Lehigh rivers. It has long been

a transportation center, first for timber rafts and Durham boats (a flat-bottomed boat that could negotiate the rapids and be poled back upstream), for the canal traffic and finally for railroads. Of interest to canal walkers is the Canal Museum (open year-round, Mon-Sat 10-4, Sun 1-5), located at the junction of the Delaware and Lehigh canals. It is in the lower end of Hugh Moore Park, which comprises the last six miles of the Lehigh Canal. The Taylor Parsons House, at 4th and Ferry Street, is a colonial residence open to the public. The Quadrant Bookstore, on 3rd Street has unusual used books and a cafe.

CANAL FEATURES—The *canal* is simply a water-filled trench with dirt banks to contain the water. There is the *towpath* bank on which you will walk and the *berm* or *heelpath* bank opposite. The *lift lock*, or simply the *lock*, is the heart of any canal system; it is designed to cope with changes in land elevation while keeping the water in the canal level and with a moderate current. While there are more exotic means to produce this effect, such as the inclined plane and tunnel, the one most frequently used is a chamber closed by gates in which the canal boats can be raised or lowered by letting water in or out. The gates are in pairs, and the most frequently used are called *miter gates*, lying in recesses in the canal sides when open. The water is let in or out by means of valves called *wickets* set in the miter gate. There were 23 lift locks all told, 19 of which you will pass. *Stop gates* can be confused with lift locks. They are single miter gates, normally left open, but which can be closed to protect the canal against excessively high water or to isolate a break in the canal. They can be distinguished by their short masonry sides and single recesses on each side for the opened gates. Lift locks are longer and have two pairs of recesses. A concrete depression in the towpath to allow flood-waters to spill out of the canal is called an *overflow*. *Waste weirs* are sluiceways built into the towpath bank to control the water level more closely than the overflow. They can be simple *sluice gates* raised and lowered by a rachet mechanism or the more complex *Taintor Gate* which can handle larger volumes of water. The former occur frequently; the latter can be seen near Locks 10, 14 and 19. If a stream crossing the canal is small, it is led under the canal bed by a *culvert* or pipe. If you look carefully you may notice some of these. For larger streams the canal is carried over on an *aqueduct*, a trough over the stream. You will cross 10 of them, a few built of wood as the initial ones were, some of concrete and others of steel beams.

Thompson-Neely

1. YARDLEY—NEW HOPE
11.5 mi (18.5 km)

This section's dramatic history centers around Washington and his army crossing the Delaware Christmas Day 1776 on their way to a brilliant and timely victory at Trenton. The two sections of Washington Crossing State Park contain much to see. It is possible to break the hike into two days by staying at Washington Crossing Inn, if you want to spend more time exploring the park than a single day will permit. The towpath in this section is a favorite for strolling, and you will meet many friendly fellow travelers doing bits of it. You can idly say that you are strolling to or from Easton! In spite of its busyness there are long stretches where you will be alone with only the canal for company.

NORTH—Leave Yardley Railroad Station and walk N on Rt 32, which runs just E of the station. Walk to Letchworth Ave, turn R and go one block to the canal. Cross the canal and go L on the towpath (here paved) for a short distance. You soon pass your first lock (Yardley Lock, No 5) with the remodeled lock keeper's house on the opposite berm. In 0.5 mi the canal passes under E Avon Ave and crosses Buck Creek over your first aqueduct. Opposite are the confused remains of mill foundations, covered by modern buildings. The towpath becomes N Edgewater Ave for about 0.2 mi, faced by small houses. At 1.6 mi you pass Lear's Lock (No 6), with the remodeled lock keeper's house opposite. Go under the approach road of Scudders Falls bridge and pass Borden's Lock (No 7) at 1.9 mi. Between here and the lower section of Washington Crossing Park is a quiet stretch, with scrub woods and farmland. Hough's Creek aqueduct comes at 3.0 mi and the Rt 532 bridge over the canal at 4.4 mi. This road forms the S boundary of the McConkey's Ferry Section of Washington Crossing State Park. Take the time to visit the museum and houses here and in the Thompson's Mill Section farther N (Tues-Sat 9-5, Sun 12-5 DST; Tues-Sat 10-4:30, Sun 12-4:30 EST; Mon closed, for both sections). To reach the park go under Rt 532 and go R, across the park to the river front. The museum is the last of the cluster of buildings running N along the river from Rt 532 and should be visited first, for orientation—a film and folder on the park.

Continuing N on the towpath, the canal remains away from the river, going through farmland and woodland, with an occasional house on the far bank. At 6.7 mi, Rt 32 recrosses the canal, and just beyond the canal goes over Jericho Creek aqueduct. At 9.1 mi you reach the Thompson's Mill Section of the park, unmistakable for its mowed lawns and picnic areas. A tall flagpole and wide terrace between the canal and river will lead you R to the Revolutionary Soldiers' graves. The only marked stone is the grave of Capt James Moore, age 24, who died Christmas Day in the nearby Thompson-Neely house. The tomb epitomized to us the sadness of war's casualties, not just for those dying young but for those left to grieve. On a more cheerful note, the Thompson-Neely house is open to visitors. Here Lord Sterling had his headquarters for the month prior to the Battle of Trenton, as his troops stood ready to prevent a British crossing of the Delaware; it was the scene of important conferences prior to the battle. On the other side of Rt 32 is Thompson's Mill, a restored gristmill (open). If you have time, a Wildflower Preserve Building, W of the mill, houses a wildlife observatory, exhibits and a bird collection set in 100 acres of a wildflower preserve.

Returning to the canal, you go 2.4 mi to New Hope. You will pass a nearly deserted large industrial building (housing a classic car showroom in 1981). In the river opposite to the building a wing dam slants across the river (probably slanting because of the underlying rock formation). The set of rapids in the opening of this dam is one of the two most dangerous on the river, claiming lives every year from unwary boaters. Just N of the building the canal widens and splits; the R fork leads to the remains of an outlet lock which allowed boats to cross the river to the Delaware-Raritan canal on the opposite shore. Cross a wooden bridge at the fork to continue on the canal towpath. The Chez Odette restaurant, once an inn for raftsmen and the canal boatmen, is here. Immediately beyond, Rt 32 recrosses the canal by the remains of Lock No 8. Here the mule-drawn barges leave for a quiet ride N on the canal, in the warmer months.

You are now in New Hope. If you stay on the towpath, you will encounter, in rapid succession, Lock No 9 with a toll collector's office (now a private residence) opposite; Dark Hollow Creek flowing into the canal with an overflow opposite; Lock No 10 with a lock keeper's house opposite; Lock No 11 (Locks 8-11 are all double locks, wide enough for two boats at once); and the aqueduct over Ingham Creek. Just beyond the aqueduct the canal is crossed by Ferry St and next Bridge St, 11.5 mi from Yardley. SOUTH—The distances in reverse are Thompson's Mill Section of Washington Crossing Park 2.4 mi; Jericho Creek aqueduct 4.8 mi; McConkey's Ferry Section of the park 7.1 mi; Lock No 7 9.6 mi; Lock No 6 9.9 mi; Letchworth Ave in Yardley 11.5 mi.

2. NEW HOPE—GOLDEN PHEASANT INN
13.1 mi (21.1 km)

In this section the canal wanders between the river and the river road, sometimes close to both, sometimes close to just one, or sometimes by itself. There is much to watch for—charming small villages, interesting old houses—with every mile bringing something new. It is the most inhabited section and has half a dozen inns scattered along its length—for elevenses, lunch, tea, dinner or to break the section into more than one day's walk.

NORTH—In New Hope the canal, about one block from the river, can be reached from any of the roads running back from the water. Once beyond the town the river road crosses the canal over Rabbit Run Bridge, and for a while the canal has only the river for company. At 1.8 mi the cluster of houses of Phillips Mill appears. You can cross over the canal from the towpath on a bridge here to visit the old gristmill (1756) R, now used for art exhibits, and the Inn. Beyond, the canal and road swing away from the river. In 0.7 mi you will pass Limeport, a former lime-burning (making) area, now no more than some stonework along the towpath. At 3.3 mi you reach Centre Bridge, where the Old York Rd (the former road

from Philadelphia to New York) crosses the river on the site of
Readings Ferry, opened in 1711. Beyond is a quiet stretch of just
the river and canal. The W bank becomes a hillside covered with
wild rhododendrons, a wall of bloom in early July. A watering
trough, for the mules which pull the barge parties from New
Hope, and picnic tables are located here, along with a water gate
(not a lock) used to isolate a section of the canal for repair. At 5.6
mi you reach Lumberton, a tiny cluster of houses to the R of the
towpath, once called "Hard Times" during a decline in business
in the early 1800s. The Cuttalossa Inn, now a restaurant, is on the
river road here, by the Cuttalossa Creek. For strong walkers or
those taking more than one day to do this section, a mile walk up
the Cuttalossa Creek road in a striking hemlock and sycamore
valley is worthwhile. Back on the canal you soon pass the defunct
Delaware Quarries, now exhibiting and selling quarried stone
from all over. You pass on the R the massive stone foundation of a
tramway that carried stone across the river to the railroad on the
Jersey side. At 6.6 mi is the village of Lumberville, named for its
sawmill operations. Cross the canal here at Lock No 12, and walk S
a few yds to visit the old-time General Store (not a museum) and a
small but good bookstore. You will pass the Tinsman
Lumberyard, run by the Tinsman family since 1869. The Black
Bass Hotel and the 1740 House are just to the S. There is a footbridge over the river here, leading to Bulls Island State Park in
New Jersey.

Continuing N, you soon pass a wing dam in the river, stone
fingers jutting from each shore, with a boiling torrent of water
between the tips. Beyond, the road, canal and river run close
together, and you will see the houses of the summer community of
Byram across the river. At 7.8 mi are Locks 13 and 14. To the R is
the Mountainside Inn (closed in 1981), one of the oldest buildings
in the area, said to have been built in 1689, now much altered.
Just N of the locks on the towpath, is a Taintor Gate. The gate is
held against the pressure of the water by a linkage that allows the
gate to open and close easily. Most water gates move stiffly in a
slot. See if you can figure out just how this one works. At 8.4 mi
Point Pleasant is L on the river road. There are an old resort hotel,
mule barns, now converted into antique shops, and the Gobbler's
Restaurant. Innisfree Inn is N, off the river road, a short distance
up Cafferty Rd. Ahead, the canal passes over the Tohickon Creek
on the longest of the canal's nine aqueducts. If you look at the
aqueduct abutments, you will note that the new aqueduct is

much narrower than the original. At 10.8 mi you will reach Smithtown and Locks 15 and 16. The latter has the largest drop on the canal. The house by the first lock was the lock keeper's house. On the towpath side is the foundation of a mule barn, used to shelter the animals while the boats were being locked through. Smithtown as a community has vanished, and the land is now held privately. Opposite, on the Jersey side, is a high ridge at the S end of which is the odd rock formation called the Devil's Tea Table. If the river is low enough, you will see Tumbling Dam Falls, a series of ledges stretching halfway across the river from the Jersey shore. At 11.8 mi you pass Lock No 17. Opposite is Treasure Island, a Boy Scout camp. Next is Marshall's Island, where Edward Marshall, of the infamous Walking Purchase, died in 1789. At 12.8 mi you go over the Tinicum Creek aqueduct and soon reach the Golden Pheasant Inn, hard by the towpath, just beyond where the river road crosses the canal.

SOUTH—For those traveling S, the distances from the Golden Pheasant Inn are Tinicum Creek aqueduct 0.3 mi; Lock No 17 1.3 mi; Locks 15 and 16 2.3 mi; Point Pleasant 4.7 mi; Locks 13 and 14 5.3 mi; Lumberville and Lock No 12 6.5 mi; Lumberton 7.5 mi; Centre Bridge 9.8 mi; Phillips Mill 11.3 mi.

3. GOLDEN PHEASANT INN—RIEGELSVILLE
13.1 mi (21.1 km)

This is the wildest section of the canal, with much of it running through woods and farmlands, away from the river road and the river. Across the canal the land is hilly, and a long stretch of it is a formidable bluff which is dramatically beautiful in any season. The canal hugs the bottom of these hills and bluffs for most of its journey here. The escarpment reaches its highest point at the Nockamixon Palisades, a somber area unreached by the winter sun and cool even on summer's hottest day. Some of the original canal settlements are still intact, suspended in time. Others are in ruins or have disappeared except for a house or two. Old inns still stand, most now restaurants or private homes. The only canal store still in operation is on this section.

NORTH—From the Golden Pheasant Inn the canal begins its turn away from the river and the river road. Here the canal flows on a high embankment above the plain which runs to the river. In 0.8 mi you come to a bridge over the canal, leading L to nearby Erwinna. This was a true canal village, having a substantial boatyard which built as well as repaired boats. The village is well kept and, except for the ubiquitous antique shops, looks much as it must have looked in the past. At 1.1 mi you come to Tinicum Park. If you are walking in early July you may come upon the Tinicum Art Festival, with all sorts of booths set up in the field N of the wooded picnic area. Look on the ground here for the large brown pods which fall from the Kentucky coffee trees. These beans were used by the Indians and the early settlers as a substitute for coffee. The tree can be recognized by its distinctive shaggy bark covered with thorny bumps. The flat land N alternates between marshes and cornland. Look for a stand of the tall elegant pampas grass, which entices many species of birds. Even on a cold winter day we were entertained by cardinals, ducks and geese as well as juncos, doves, flickers and a downy woodpecker. At 2.5 mi in Uhlerstown the sight of the only covered bridge over the canal will delight you. The bridge has been in continuous use since it was built in 1832 and is a good example of bridge building of that era.

Uhlerstown grew up under the entrepreneurship of Michael Uhler. The original buildings still stand but now serve different functions. There is the iron-balconied old hotel, the Uhler mansion, a general store with a hoist for raising material to the upper floor and the ruins of a limekiln. The building where canal boats

164

were built, just S of the limekilns, is now a private home. You may want to see how many of these you can identify. The usual remodeled lock keeper's house and mule sheds will by now be readily recognizable canal features. Uhlerstown Lock (No 18) is beyond the bridge. Between here and Lodi Lock the canal runs close to steep red cliffs. Notice a small earth dike on the far side of the canal, built to protect the canal from the inevitable showers of stones coming off these cliffs. At 3.4 mi is Lodi Lock (No 19). You don't think of the canal having much current until you come to a place where a stream flows into it as here. It had rained the day before we came and then had turned bitterly cold. The spray from the swollen stream had frozen into a delicate lace ruffle of ice under which the water poured into the lock. At 5.8 mi you will come to the lower border of the village of Upper Black Eddy, named for a large eddy in the river here where the raftsmen brought in their unwieldy rafts for the night. You will shortly come to the only remaining canal store still open for business, serving the village but unknown to passing motorists on the river road. At 6.6 mi the river road crosses the canal and you leave the village behind.

The canal now runs by itself for several miles. This is a quiet area of farmland returning to forest. At 8.8 mi you reach the Indian Rock Hotel, now a restaurant but formerly the Narrows Hotel much used by boatmen. There is a convenient footbridge to it. The road and canal now run directly under the highest section of the cliffs, which for the next few miles are called the Nockamixon Palisades, rising to 500 ft in places. In winter the cliffs are festooned in ice cascades that rival the arctic, sheets of white that writhe down ravines and gullies. This section is sunless during the winter months and shady for most of the day even in summer.

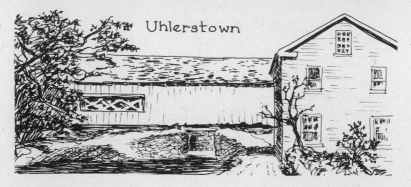

Uhlerstown

Kentucky
coffee tree

However, in the green seasons the cliffs are gentled by small trees and shrubs which find rootholds in the sheer rock. At 9.7 mi you reach the Narrowsville Lock (No 20). In past years a hamlet thrived here, but now the houses have all disappeared except for one. The small amount of land between the river and cliffs is taken up by the canal and road, yet there was a large gristmill by the river's edge, a large house under the cliff opposite the lock and several other houses. At 9.9 mi the canal goes over Gallows Run (pleasant name!) on an aqueduct and at 10.3 mi reaches Kintnersville. Most of the village is away from the canal but you will pass a few houses.

For the next 1.5 mi there is space for farmland between the canal and the river. A paved road runs on the towpath side, and there are scattered white-painted wooden houses along it. This road soon crosses the canal to the river road (here Rt 611). At the canal bridge is a handsome redstone farmhouse, and on its lawn, just by the towpath, is a small stone building with a chimney, one window and a door over which is the date 1831. This is about the time the canal opened, and the little house may have been for a canal maintenance worker. At 12.0 mi you reach Durham Furnace, heralded by a large white house (once an inn but now a private dwelling), then a cluster of smaller houses, an aqueduct over Durham or Cooke Creek and Durham Lock (No 21). No trace remains of the busy iron-making community started here in 1698. The remains of the Durham Cave, a famous attraction even during colonial times but largely destroyed for its limestone, lie across the road on the N side of the creek. The Durham boats, used on the river before the canal was built to float goods downstream to market, were made here. Washington and his army were ferried across the river on their way to the Battle of Trenton in these craft, examples of which may be seen at Washington Crossing Park (see Section 1). The canal continues uneventfully until Riegelsville (13.1 mi). Here a road bridge crosses the canal and leads to a Roebling steel suspension bridge across the river, built in 1903. The Riegelsville Hotel is by the bridge, its backyard abutting the towpath.

4. RIEGELSVILLE—EASTON
8.2 mi (13.2 km)

This short section has a feeling of being "up-country," of an ambience near the turn of the century. The village houses are more modest, their owners work locally, and life cannot be too different than that of the 1920s when the canal was coming to the end of its 100-year life. The farms are the principal livelihood of their owners and not of "gentlemen" farmers. The surroundings seem quieter, in spite of the busy river road that plays hide-and-seek with the canal on this section. On summer weekends the northern part is fairly well tramped by day walkers from Easton, but the rest of the time the towpath is deserted except for abundant bird life. Easton will appear all too soon, if you have come N, but the Canal Museum and a restored stretch of the Lehigh Canal are there to entertain you.

NORTH—Leaving the Riegelsville Hotel by its backyard, you will find the town continuing along the river road for nearly a mile before its northern limit is reached (footbridge here). The road and the houses are well away from the canal. You see a handsome church spire, affording a distinguished landmark coming S. A slough or slack water soon appears beyond the berm bank, running parallel to the canal. At 1.0 mi is Stop Gate No 7, still operable. The gate differs from the usual by being a single drop gate which, when open, lies horizontal on the bottom of the canal. A sluiceway with its valve is beside the drop gate opening and is used to equalize the water level if the gate is in the up position and is to be dropped. The winch and chain for raising and lowering the gate is still in place between the gate opening and the sluiceway. Beyond the gate is a Taintor Gate and concrete spillway in the towpath bank.

The road, canal and river soon run close together, the towpath bank separated from the river by a protecting stone and concrete wall. At 1.7 mi you reach Fry's Run aqueduct, the shortest and

mitre gate

last of the 10 aqueducts on the canal. From here to the next lock the river and canal make a large S-curve, with the river road running above. A lonely stone bridge pier stands at the head of an island in the middle of the river, the other piers and the bank abutments for the bridge having vanished completely. At 2.7 mi are the Ground Hog Locks (Nos 22-23). Originally two single-width locks it is now one double-width lock capable of taking two canal boats side by side. It had a pair of miter gates at the lower end, now disintegrated; a single drop gate at the upper end, still in place; and a second drop gate beyond it, closed only when repairs to the lock are necessary. A small house, the "wicket shanty," by the upper gate contains the mechanism for operating the wickets (valves) and the drop gate. The lock has the highest lift on the canal (17.3 ft). The large building by the river, fed by water from a diversion channel from the canal, once housed a hydroelectric plant for the trolley that ran along the river here. The lock tenders house, still in its original condition is above the diversion. Just N of the lock is the site of the Raubsville Paper Company, started by Peter Uhler as a distillery but converted for making paper after the Civil War. It ended its career by a fiery death in 1930. At 3.3 mi you reach Raubsville, a village of modest houses of great architectural variety, with interesting backyards. The village straggles along the river road for a considerable distance. You soon cross an overflow and reach the northern limit of the village at a footbridge, which serves two houses on the riverbank.

For the next 4.0 mi the road and canal separate and rejoin a number of times. In places the embankment of the old trolley line that ran from Doylestown to Easton can be seen on the far side of the road. This line operated for the first quarter of this century and afforded a leisurely and scenic trip. The abutments of its bridges over the small streams flowing into the river and the platforms for its stations can be seen by a quick eye. At about 6.0 mi you will pass the Black Horse Tavern (1782) up on the river road, a good lunch stop. A little beyond is an odd concrete structure at the canalside. Its function seems to be to load and discharge some kind of material, perhaps into the canal boats. Next are two stop gates about 0.5 mi apart, the last on the canal. The buildings of Phillipsburg will begin to appear on the opposite side of the river, with Mt Parnassus as a precursor, a distinctive bare hump of rock. A network of three railroad bridges herald the end of the canal. As you pass under the last bridge you reach the last lock (No 24), beyond which is the Lehigh River's confluence with the Delaware.

By this guard lock (so called because it protected the canal from high water in the Lehigh) is the remains of a weigh lock, in which the tonnage of the canal boats and hence their canal fees were determined. The Lehigh is dammed here to provide water for the first stage of the Lehigh Canal. By the river road is the Canal Museum, a must to visit (year-round, Mon-Sat 10-4, Sun 1-5). Leave the canal here, walk N along Rt 611 and in a few yds cross the Lehigh to Easton. Turn R and walk along the bank of the Lehigh and then the Delaware to the first bridge over the Delaware (Northampton St). Turn L here and pass, in short order, Hotel Easton and the bus depot. The Sheraton Hotel is near the bridge you took over the Lehigh.

A section of the Lehigh Canal has been restored just W of the end of the Delaware Canal, and if you have energy remaining, you can continue your walk for another 3.2 mi from the museum. Walk N on Rt 611 and cross to Canal St just before the bridge over the Lehigh. Beyond the railroad a path leads down to the towpath along the river. At 0.8 mi you reach the outlet lock to the canal proper, with remains of the Collector's Office of the Lehigh Coal and Navigation Company. At 1.0 mi is Abbott St Lock, site of a former industrial area. At 2.3 mi is the Old Glendon Bridge area, where pedalboats and canoes can be rented and where a mule-drawn canal boat, the *Josiah White*, will take you for an hour-long ride (Memorial Day-Labor Day, Wed-Sun; Sept, Sat-Sun). At 3.2 mi is the Lock Tender's House, whose ground floor is now a museum showing how a lock tender and his family lived in the 1800s (Memorial Day-Labor Day, Wed, Thurs, Sat, Sun 1-4).

Raubsville

SHENANDOAH WALK
Virginia, 4 days, 39.1 miles (63.1 km)

SECTION	DISTANCE		OVERNIGHT POINTS
1	13.2 mi	(21.3 km)	Elkton-Lewis Mountain
2	8.9 mi	(14.4 km)	Lewis Mountain-Big Meadow
3	7.9 mi	(12.7 km)	Big Meadow-Skyland
4	9.1 mi	(14.7 km)	Skyland-Luray
2a	9.3 mi	(15.0 km)	Stanley-Big Meadow
4a	10.4 mi	(16.8 km)	Skyland Circuit Hike

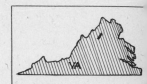

MAP—

PATC Map No 10, Shenandoah National Park, Central Section. Order from the Potomac Appalachian Trail Club, 1718 N St NW, Washington, DC 20036.

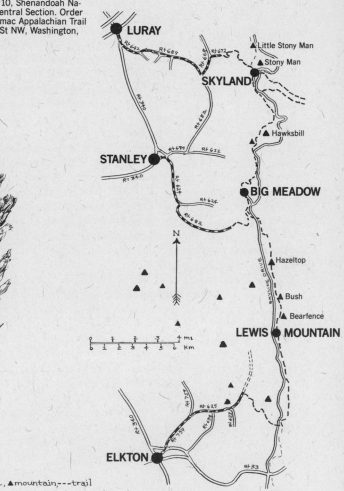

Key: ● place, ▲ mountain, --- trail

TRANSPORTATION
Luray
Stanley—bus (Trailways/Quick-Livick), Front Royal & Washington
Elkton—1 r/t Mon-Fri

ACCOMMODATIONS
Write or phone ARA Virginia Skyline Co., Inc., PO Box 191 Luray, VA 22835 703-743-5108
Skyland (early April-early Nov)
Big Meadow (late May-late Oct)
Lewis Mt (late May-late Oct)

Our most southerly Walk climbs to and runs along the high spine of the magnificent Blue Ridge Mountains. There are frequent sweeping views from lookout points, west across the beautiful Shenandoah Valley and east to the wooded hollows of the Rapidan. The trail starts and ends in the Shenandoah Valley at small towns along a bus route. It winds past farm holdings and on old woods roads that once carried wagon traffic over the mountain ridge. The ridge hiking is on easy but scenic sections of the Appalachian Trail.

Most of the Walk is in the Shenandoah National Park. Once the home of mountain people who settled here in the mid-1700s, the land, lumbered for its hemlocks and other trees and cleared for farming, gradually became less productive and the people began to drift away. When the park was established in 1925 the few remaining people were moved to new communities in the valleys. Nature has now healed the scars of man's exploitation, and the past occupation is seen only in the tumbled stone walls, an occasional old apple tree or a collection of gravestones. You will probably see white-tailed deer, especially in the mornings and evenings; they are protected in the park and therefore very tame.

Signs say that this is bear country, and there are indeed a number of bruins. However, only the unwary tent and trailer campers who do not put away their food are likely to encounter any. The most visible bird is the turkey buzzard always soaring overhead, and it will often be joined by the crow-like raven, seen this far south only on the ridges of the Appalachians. You can distinguish it from a crow by its bulk (twice crow size), its soaring flight, and above all by its distinctive croak rather than caw. An occasional grouse or quail will flash away through the woods, startling you by the whirr of its wings. Smaller birds are abundant. Poisonous snakes will be seen once in a great while, but they are very shy. Just be careful to look before you sit!

OVERNIGHT POINTS

All the places at which you stay the night are on the Skyline Drive. Each place has its own flavor since each was built at different times. **Lewis Mountain** is a campground with a few fully equipped cabins as well as tenting and trailer areas. You will have to provide your own food, but there is a campground store. **Big Meadow** has a large lodge, restaurant and surrounding cabin bedrooms. **Skyland** is similar to Big Meadow, but much older. Predating the park, it received guests by carriage from Luray in the late 1800s.

These areas are oases of civilized catering along a stretch of wilderness. The designers of both the Skyline Drive and the three lodgings have done an excellent job of fitting into the natural setting, leaving the mountain much as the Indians found it.

1. ELKTON—LEWIS MOUNTAIN
13.2 mi (21.3 km)/2600 ft (790 m)

This is a fairly long hike up to and along the Shenandoah ridge. You have about five miles of easy walking from Elkton on back roads through farmlands of the Shenandoah Valley, with evidences of prosperity shown by new houses and barns. You enter the woods at the steep slope leading to the ridge and struggle not quite three miles up a fire road. Once on the ridge the gradients are easy. You climb two mountains (Baldface and Lewis), but neither rise much above the ridge's average of 3000 feet. You pass through a now-wooded flat with the unusual name of Kites Deadening. A deadening is an area in which the trees were killed by ringing, i.e., removing the bark around the base; crops were then planted among the dead trees. This saved the time and effort to remove the trees. There are occasional views. The way is well marked and the footing excellent.

172

NORTH—From the center of Elkton on Rt 340 walk E on Rockingham Rd and pick up the sign for Rt 759 on the edge of town. Follow this route through farmland and reach the junction with Rt 625 at 2.6 mi. Go straight ahead on Rt 625 (Rt 759 goes L). At the end of the paved road (4.6 mi) Rt 623 comes in on R. Continue ahead on a dirt road, entering woods in 0.5 mi and climbing to a small saddle at 5.7 mi. Here the dirt Dry Run Falls Fire Rd goes R, blazed yellow. It climbs, steeply at times, to the high ridge, crosses the Skyline Dr and meets the Appalachian Trail (AT), blazed white, 8.5 mi from Elkton. Go L (N) on the AT and begin a long easy climb up Baldface Mt to its summit (3600 ft, 10.1 mi). Descend gently for 0.8 mi to the flat Kites Deadening, then steeply by switchbacks for a short distance, and cross the Pocosin Fire Rd at 11.4 mi. At 12.5 mi you begin to climb Lewis Mt and reach a post and trail L at 13.2 mi leading 100 yds to Lewis Mt Campground.

SOUTH—From the S end of Lewis Mt Campground take the Lewis Mt Trail a short distance E to the AT, blazed white, and follow the NORTH directions in reverse. Your mileages are Pocosin Fire Rd 1.8 mi; Kites Deadening 2.3 mi; Baldface Mt 3.1 mi; South River Fire Rd 4.8 mi (go R and it becomes the Dry Falls Run Fire Rd, blazed yellow); Rt 625 (dirt, unmarked) 7.6 mi; Rt 759 10.6 mi.

2. LEWIS MOUNTAIN—BIG MEADOW
8.9 mi (14.4 km)/550 ft (170 m)

This is a pleasant ridge hike on the Appalachian Trail. Although some of it is located close to the Skyline Drive, you are miraculously shielded from its sight and traffic noises. The trail goes over two mountaintops, Hazeltop and Bearfence. The exciting part of the day is going through the Bearfence Mt area with its glorious views and dramatic rocky bearfence. You can usually count on seeing some four-legged creatures during the hike as well as the two-legged kind you always see on weekends and holidays.

It is always a good route for wild flowers; look for plentiful patches of hepatica in the early spring and for gentians in late summer.

You will pass a side trail that leads down to Camp Hoover, President Herbert Hoover's retreat on the Rapidan River. He deeded it to the federal government at the end of his term, and it is now under the supervision of the Park Service. It is presently used as a retreat for members of government. Its hidden location and difficult access make it ideal for that purpose. The path for all of the hike is graded and well maintained, and the way is well marked and easy to follow. The elevation gained is modest, but there are a few short steep pitches.

NORTH—The AT runs just E of the cabins, campground and picnic area of Lewis Mt. You can reach it by walking through the woods or by taking one of several short trails from the picnic area. Go N (L) on this white-blazed trail. In a mile you cross a dirt road; 200 ft R is the Bearfence Mt Shelter and just L is Skyline Dr. The trail soon becomes a wide lane with soft pine needles underfoot until you commence the climb up Bearfence Mt. The ascent goes by switchbacks across the S face through stands of laurel and pine. Near the top you will get grand views E and S of forested hills and hollows. A figure-eight side trail here leads over the rocks of Bearfence Mt. The first (southerly) loop R climbs the rock barrier easily and is a must if you hanker after far views. It affords a magnificent sweep of the woods, farms and villages of the Shenandoah Valley to the W, quite different from the wilder view you had before to the E. The northerly loop, a strenuous hands-and-knees scramble over the rough rocks, is for the agile and venturesome. When you descend from the rocky ridge back to the AT, you will discover that the metaphor "bearfence" is quite fitting; the rocks form a dramatic barrier, which towers up like a gigantic jagged fence.

From Bearfence Mt, the trail stays fairly level for 1.5 mi through an attractive woods setting. It comes close to the Skyline Dr in places, but you will scarcely be conscious of it. At 3.5 mi from Lewis Mt you cross the fire road at Booten Gap, and in another 0.5 mi the Laurel Prong Trail comes in on your R. You stay on the AT, reaching the wooded summit of Hazeltop (3812 ft) by a gentle climb. Hazeltop is the AT's highest point in the park, but there is no feeling here of crossing over a mountain. We found the blazes on the ascent to be quite far apart and were a little unsure we were going right. However, there are no side trails to lure you off, so just follow the well-traveled way.

174

The trail on to Milam Gap (3257 ft) is a relatively featureless path through brambles and shrublike hazel trees. The tedium can be broken by feasting your stomach on the berries in the summer and your eye on the gentians and asters in the late summer or the brilliant foliage in the fall. At 6.2 mi you cross the Skyline Dr and at 7.3 mi the Tanners Ridge Fire Rd (yellow blazes). Beyond you will cross a meadow with a small graveyard L. Looking back, you will have a fine view of Hazeltop. You may see deer feeding here. Soon you cross two bridle paths and go through an oak forest. After crossing a service road, the trail goes along the W side of the ridge. There are occasional rocky viewpoints of the western valley. At 8.3 mi a side trail R leads in 0.1 mi to the Black Rock Viewpoint and on to Big Meadow Lodge in another 0.2 mi. If you continue on the AT, you will pass under the cliffs of Black Rock and reach another short side trail to the lodge at 8.8 mi.

SOUTH—Go around the N end of the Big Meadow Lodge on a short trail W down to the AT (blazed white), and go L (S). Your mileage points are Black Rock cliffs 0.3 mi; Tanners Ridge Fire Rd 1.5 mi; Skyline Dr crossing and Milam Gap 2.6 mi; Hazeltop 4.5 mi; Laurel Prong Trail 5.0 mi; Booten Gap 5.4 mi; Bearfence Mt Loop trails 7.0 mi; Bearfence Mt Shelter 7.9 mi; Lewis Mt Campground 8.9 mi.

Bearfence

3. BIG MEADOW—SKYLAND
7.9 mi (12.7 km)/700 ft (210 m)
This section of the Appalachian Trail in the Shenandoah Park features rugged cliffs to walk above, below and across on ledges. There are frequent sweeping views of the woods and farms of the Shenandoah Valley. The many cliffs are of greenstone, made from a series of lava flows which once covered the area. The woods through which you pass are mostly oak and hickory, with an occasional hemlock stand. In elevations above 3500 feet you will find,

however, trees which normally grow only in the Canadian Zone—balsam fir, red spruce and grey birch. The footing is excellent, the gradient easy and the way well blazed.

An amusing incident happened to us while hiking this section. It is our habit to leave (unobtrusively) our biodegradable leftovers to enrich the soil and feed small creatures. When the leftovers come in bright orange skins they must be well concealed. While lifting a rock for this purpose after lunch, a glimpse of a shiny red and black body meant only one thing to us—copperhead! We were content with a "sorry, go back to sleep," but our son insisted on seeing it. So, with elaborate precautions, we tipped the rock over with a long stick, only to uncover, not a coiled poisonous snake, but an innocuous newt to whom we apologized and went our way chagrinned. Although a newt rather than a snake is what you are likely to find when turning over a stone, the experience did remind us that carefree actions of this kind are not good practice where there are poisonous snakes. So take care when disturbing the ground cover or choosing a place to sit.

NORTH—Walk around the N end of the Big Meadow Lodge on a path going W downhill. In a short distance you reach the AT (blazed white); go R (N). The trail winds downhill past the campground and amphitheater (R). You soon go over a small knob, the Monkey Head, and in another mile you go by a house-sized split rock (R) and reach a spur trail (1.5 mi) leading R to the Fisher Gap Overlook on the Skyline Dr. Continue N on the AT, crossing the Red Gate Fire Rd in 0.1 mi. You soon go under the Franklin Cliffs, on a ledge above more cliffs high above the forest, and continue along the W side of the main ridge. At 3.5 mi you pass a small open area rapidly being overgrown with pine and locust. At 3.8 mi you reach a sag between Nakedtop and Hawksbill mts. Here an unmarked trail leads R 0.9 mi to the top of Hawksbill (4050 ft), the highest point in the park. This trail rejoins the AT at Hawksbill Gap and adds 0.5 mi and 700 ft to your hike. Continuing from the sag on the AT, you pass underneath cliffs and scree slopes, with good views of the valley below. At Hawksbill Gap (4.8 mi, 3361 ft) a trail leads R 100 yds to the Skyline Dr and the other end of the Hawksbill Mt Trail. At 5.3 mi the trail goes under the cliffs of Crescent Rock, similar to the Franklin Cliffs, with good views W. At 6.0 mi there is a piped spring on the R by the trail. You now climb toward the top of the ridge through stands of laurel, blooming in early June, and reach Pollock Knob (6.6 mi, 3560 ft). At 7.3 mi you pass the Skyland stables and at 7.9 mi reach the Skyland parking lot.

SOUTH—Leave the Skyland dining room and go S through the parking lot to a post with the AT symbol and white blaze. Follow the AT to Big Meadow. The mileages are Pollock Knob 1.3 mi; Crescent Rock cliffs 2.7 mi; Hawksbill Gap 3.1 mi; sag between Hawksbill and Nakedtop 4.1 mi; Franklin Cliffs 6.0 mi; Fisher Gap 6.3 mi; Big Meadow Lodge 7.9 mi.

4. SKYLAND—LURAY
9.1 mi (14.7 km)/2800 ft (850 m)
This is a two-part hike, down through woods on the steep slope of the Shenandoah ridge by an old carriage road and then along the gentle slope of the fertile valley of the Shenandoah River. The route on the forested slope is on the old Skyland Road over which the Victorians were driven in carriages to Skyland Lodge. The road climbs 2000 feet; you can imagine as you hike the struggle the horses must have had getting the carriages up. Perhaps a kind-hearted coachman made his passengers walk the steeper bits! The road follows a spur of the main ridge between a hollow and a deep ravine, and there are good views all the way. Although the road was made for wheeled vehicles, there is no evidence of them now on the soft unmarked track.

At the woods edge there are old weathered buildings, well kept but unspoiled by modernization. We had the feeling as we passed that we should knock at the door and ask if we could just tarry a day or two and soak up the peace and contentment which we felt all around us.

The way is easy to find and the footing excellent.

NORTH—From in front of the dining hall at Skyland, go N on the AT, blazed white, first on a paved path and then a woods trail; cross a paved road at 0.2 mi and reach the old dirt Skyland Rd at 0.3 mi. Go L, passing a gate and picking up yellow blazes. The

road goes downhill on the ridge between Dry Run Hollow and
Kettle Canyon. At 3.2 mi from the AT you pass a second gate and
the road becomes Rt 672. Beyond the gate 0.6 mi you reach the
paved Rt 668. Go L 0.9 mi, now in farmland, to Rt 689, and go R.
When this route turns R in 2.0 mi, keep straight ahead on Rt 642
for 1.6 mi to Rt 340. Go R 0.5 mi to the center of Luray.
SOUTH—Walk S on Rt 340 from Luray. About 0.5 mi from town
center, soon after you pass under a railroad bridge, take Rt 642 L.
In 1.6 mi it joins Rt 689 and in another 2.0 mi you go L on Rt 668.
Take this 0.9 mi to Rt 672, 5.0 mi from Luray. Go R on Rt 672,
passing through a gate in 0.5 mi, and ascend the old Skyland Rd,
blazed yellow, to the AT. Go R on the AT, blazed white, 0.3 mi to
Skyland.

The route sounds complicated with all its turns but is
straightforward as you walk it. The map we recommend will help
keep you on the road.

2a. STANLEY—BIG MEADOW
9.3 mi (15.0 km)/2500 ft (760 m)
This is another way to reach the Blue Ridge summits. It leaves Rt
340 at Stanley and goes through rolling farmland and woods,
mostly on quiet back roads. The countryside has a mixture of old
farmhouses, ancient barns and new houses. It is a steady gradient
all the way, making it very easy to gain or lose the considerable
altitude between the valley and the ridge.

We have included this additional way to the ridge so that you
can shorten the Walk to three days or keep it to four days if you
want to take the Whiteoak Canyon-Cedar Run circuit hike from
Skyland (see Section 4a).
EAST—Walk N on Rt 340 from the center of Stanley to Rt 689,
and go R for 0.6 mi to its junction with Rt 624. Go R (S) on Rt 624
for 2.5 mi to Rt 682. Go R uphill on Rt 682 to its end 6.7 mi from
Stanley at the boundary of Shenandoah Park (locked gate here).
Ahead is the wide Tanners Ridge Fire Rd, blazed yellow. Go 1.4
mi on the fire road to the AT (7.8 mi, blazed white). There is a
small cemetery here still being used for burials. Go L (N) on the
AT, crossing horse trails and a service road in the next 0.5 mi. At
8.8 mi a trail goes R 0.1 mi to Black Rock Viewpoint and on to Big
Meadow Lodge, 0.2 mi farther., You can take this trail or continue
on the AT, passing under the cliffs of Black Rock. At 9.3 mi on
the AT you pass below the lodge; there is a short path R to it.

WEST—From Big Meadow Lodge go W to the AT (blazed white) running just below the lodge. Go L (S) for 1.5 mi to the Tanners Ridge Fire Rd, blazed yellow. Go R (W) down this wide dirt road to Rt 682 at the park boundary (2.6 mi), then to Rt 624 mi (6.2 mi), Rt 689 (8.7 mi) and Stanley (9.3 mi). Town center is L (S).

4a. SKYLAND—CIRCUIT HIKE (WHITEOAK CANYON-CEDAR RUN)

10.4 mi (16.8 km) / 2350 ft (720 m)

It would be a shame, once you are in the park, for you to miss one of its most spectacular and popular hikes. Not for the weak-kneed, this hike follows the park's two deepest and steepest canyons, filled with waterfalls and cascades. The trail drops 2350 feet to the valley floor before climbing laboriously back up to the ridge. The Whiteoak Run, in its rush to the valley, has cut six cascades, each more than 40 feet high. Its canyon is lined with tall trees, mostly oak, hemlock, tulip and ash. The Cedar Run is equally precipitous but with fewer falls and cascades. The hike is worth an extra day; if you can spare only four days, you may cut out the sections from Lewis Mountain and Elkton (Sections 1 and 2) and come into Big Meadow from Stanley (Section 2a). We describe travel in one direction only.

EAST—Walk out the S entrance of Skyland to the Skyline Dr. The Whiteoak Canyon Trail starts at a parking area on the E side of the drive almost directly across from the entrance. The trail is well worn and well blazed (blue), so there is little danger of going astray. You drop gently at first, crossing a branch of Whiteoak Run at 0.5 mi and the Old Rag Fire Rd beyond. At 0.8 mi the Limberlost Trail comes in on the R. You soon enter the canyon,

179

and the way steepens. At 2.2 mi the trail goes sharply R and crosses the run by a footbridge. A few feet farther, the Big Meadow Horse Trail intersects. (You may short-circuit the climb by going W 1.8 mi on the horse trail back to Skyline Dr only 0.6 mi from the upper end of Cedar Run Trail.) Continue downhill. At 2.3 mi there is a good view of the first of the six cascades in the canyon.

Now the trail descends very steeply over rocks. In 0.1 mi a spur leads to the base of the first cascade. At 3.7 mi you cross a side creek (a waterfall is visible from here) and come close to the run just below the last cascade. At 4.3 mi the Cedar Run Trail goes R, fording the Whiteoak Run. Blazed blue also but not signposted, it is not easy to miss as it is well worn. Leave the Whiteoak Canyon Trail here and follow the Cedar Run Trail which runs nearly level for about a mile. Ford Cedar Run at 5.2 mi and begin to climb. At 6.0 mi you reach Cedar Run's highest falls and across the run loom the perpendicular Half Mile Cliffs. The trail soon crosses the stream and swings away from it for awhile, still climbing. At 6.7 mi you pass the uppermost cascade, and the gradient eases off. At 7.6 mi a spur leads 100 yds to a shelter. Continue ahead to the Skyline Dr and cross to the Hawksbill Gap Lookout parking area. To the R of a sign displaying the trails in this area, a trail goes W downhill a short distance to the AT. Go R on the AT 0.4 mi to a trail R, signposted "Crescent Rock Overlook." (You can continue on the AT to Skyland, but this would be covering the trail you did yesterday or will do tomorrow.) Instead go R on the Crescent Rock Trail to the Overlook. Walk out the N entrance of the Overlook, cross Skyline Dr and pick up the Crescent Rock Trail just S. Follow the trail on an easy downhill gradient for 1.1 mi until it ends in the Limberlost Trail. Go L on this trail for 0.4 mi to where it ends at the Old Rag Fire Rd. Go R 0.2 mi on the fire road to its intersection with the Whiteoak Canyon Trail and you are nearly back to where you started. Go L uphill on the Whiteoak Canyon Trail for 0.6 mi to the entrance to Skyland. It is rather strenuous but quite rewarding.

hepatica

NOTES

A. TRANSPORTATION AND ACCOMMODATIONS

This note supplements the material on transportation and accommodations contained in the second page of each Walk.

PUBLIC TRANSPORTATION—Nothing seems, at this writing, more uncertain than the future of the U.S. mass transportation system. What we include is correct as of the fall of 1981, but schedules may change and lines may be discontinued entirely. You will need to write or call for current schedules to the bus company, railroad or airline that we indicate as serving a Walk.

Our stressing public transportation to and from the Walks is not primarily to woo you from your love affair with the auto, an addiction most of us share, but to free you from its embrace where it becomes too inconvenient. Most of our Walks go from point A to point B (only four are circuit routes), and hikers with only one car have a generally difficult problem leaving the car at A and getting back to it at B (it has been done with the help of friendly innkeepers, but that is the exception and not the rule). We own up to urging public transportation for another less immediate but ultimately more compelling reason—the uncertain future and cost of gasoline supply. We aim to show that it is possible to lead the good life (meaning wilderness hiking) even if you cannot get or afford gasoline.

One last unhappy thought on the car. More and more, experience and the police are telling us not to leave cars unattended in remote areas because of vandalism and theft. Deploring it does not make it any less so, but using public transportation does.

Almost all the trailheads are served by bus, and thankful we are for that flexible and pervasive form of transport. Wherever you live in the U.S., you can get to and from our routes by bus alone. However, we love to ride on trains, so we mention them whenever it is possible to use them. It is rarely possible to use that epitome of comfortable travel, the sleeper, to a Walk, but if the Montrealer is still running, you can leave Washington, Philadelphia or New York after work and arrive the next morning, reasonably rested, near the Mansfield Walk (at Waterbury, Vermont). Less dramatic are the trains that can take you in the daylight hours, at least partway, on your journey to and from a walk.

The airlines, of course, can take you great distances in a hurry but will generally land you neither near your destination nor close to most other means of public transportation. We have found one exception, the airport limousine, that may for a fairly reasonable fee deliver you right to the trailhead. The larger the group, the less the per capita price; even a small group of three or four lowers the cost greatly. Arranging for a pickup at the end of the Walk is another matter because of the uncertainties of when and where you may emerge from the forest and how payment is to be guaranteed. With good will on both sides and advance payment, much can be done however.

The ubiquitous taxi may be the only answer, in some cases, for connecting the Walks with scheduled transportation. It is more widely available than the airport limousine but suffers from the same limitations. Before you set off in one be sure you know the costs, either as a flat rate or on a per mile basis.

For each route the type, name and generally frequency of ser-·vice from the nearest major transportation center is given: for example, "Big Indian—bus (Adirondack Trailways) New York, 5 r/t dly." Sometimes this routing is more extensive, where feeder lines and main routes are given, or where more than one type of transportation is given.

We list below the full name, the address and/or telephone number of all the transportation companies mentioned in this book. If you are using airlines or Amtrak for part of your journey, any travel agency will arrange the booking for you and save you a deal of trouble.

Bus Lines

Adirondack Trailways, 411 Washington Ave, Kingston, NY 12401 914-339-4230 (Kingston), 518-436-8411 (Albany), 212-564-8484 (NYC)

Bonanza Bus Lines, 27 Sabin Ave, PO Box 1116, Annex Station, Providence, RI 02901 401-331-7500

Cape Cod Bus Lines, 11 Walker St, Falmouth, MA 02540 617-548-0333

Concord Trailways, S Main St, Concord, NH 03301 603-224-3381

Englander Coach, PO Box 631, N Adams, MA 01247 413-662-2016

Greyhound, Greyhound Towers, Phoenix, AZ 85077 602-248-5000

Mohawk Coach Lines, Inc, PO Box 186, Rt 46 Elmwood Park, NJ 07407 201-777-1212

Quick-Livick Inc, 708 C St, Staunton, VA 24401

Red and Tan Lines (Rockland Coach), 126 N Washington Ave, Bergenfield, NJ 07621 201-385-8480

Short Line (Hudson Transit) 17 Franklin Turnpike, Mahwah, NJ
  07430 201-529-3666
Transport of NJ, 180 Boyden Ave, Maplewood, NJ 07040
  201-761-8337
Trailways (Nat'l Trailways Bus System), 1200 Eye St NW, Washington, DC 20005 202-737-5820
Vermont Transit, 135 St Paul St, Burlington, VT 05401
  802-862-9671
Warwick Stage, 60 Galloway Rd, Warwick, NY 10990
  914-986-3322 (NY), 800-772-2222 (NJ)

Airlines
Provincetown-Boston Airline 617-487-0240 (P-town)
                             617-567-6090 (Boston)
Bar Harbor Airline   800-432-7854

Railroads
Amtrak—800-562-5380
Septa—215-329-4800 (if no answer, call 800-462-0920)

Boats
Provincetown—Provincetown Steamship Co, 20 Long Wharf,
  Boston, MA 02110, 617-723-7800

PUBLIC ACCOMMODATIONS—We provide in each section the
names, addresses and telephone numbers of places to stay.
Generally, the places listed are *all* those available which are easily
reached by foot from the trail. In the few cases where more than
three lodgings are available at an overnight point, we will list
three and note where to write to find out about the others. We do
not rate any accommodations but will not include any in obvious-
ly poor physical condition (a rarity on our routes, we are pleased to
add). If the lodgings are not by the trail, we specify the distance
and direction in the trail description. For example, "The
Cranberry Inn is 0.5 mi L from the trail head on Rt 3."
  Do *not* start on a Walk without getting places to stay
beforehand. You may be used to casual car traveling, where you
pick up lodgings as the spirit moves you and are willing and able
to travel miles if your first choices are full. With us you will be
afoot; an extra mile is a burden and an extra 15 miles is un-
thinkable. So arrange ahead for lodgings. If you are delayed by
weather, illness or mountain foot (a strange reluctance to put one
foot in front of the other!), it is a kindness to let your next-night
innkeeper know you will not be there. Most of our accommoda-

tions are small places, so that an empty room which could have been filled hurts.

You will encounter a wide variety of "comfortable places" on our routes. They range from restored old inns catering to the carriage trade, such as the charming dozen scattered along the Delaware Canal Walk, to the austere but friendly AMC huts of the Presidential Range Walk. All accommodations which we list provide meals or are in easy walking distance of a restaurant.

B. TRAILKEEPING

Keeping to the trails we have chosen requires no prior experience in wilderness travel; all are well marked and maintained. Because they are some of the more interesting, many are visibly well trodden. They frankly are pretty hard to lose. However, you do need to know the basics of blazing. Almost all your trails will be marked at intervals (100-200 yds apart on average) by either blazes painted on trees or rocks or metal or plastic markers fastened to trees. Both will be a specific color, a great aid where trails intersect. These blazes are often high above the ground to be visible at a distance or to avoid being covered by deep snow. They may be one of several shapes, but will stay a specific shape and color on a specific trail. A day's hike may follow one or a sequence of several different blazes. We call out the color and, if the shape is other than oblong, the shape in our detailed trail description.

A further convention adopted throughout the eastern U.S. is the use of a double blaze, generally one above the other, to indicate a turn in the trail. It is especially needed where the trail leaves a road and enters the woods. It sometimes appears when not needed; put that down to the exuberance of the blaze painter.

If at any time you find you no longer see blazes, don't just bull ahead; backtrack until you pick up the blazes again. Losing blazes seems to happen most frequently when you are on an old woods road and the trail turns off.

In the very few instances where our routes take you away from blazes—generally to get to your night's lodging or to public transportation—it is either obvious from the context, or we will note the fact in the detailed trail description.

Trails on private lands are frequently relocated because of housing developments or the misbehavior of a few hikers. You may encounter such a relocation, put in place after this book was researched (1981), and find the actual trail at variance with our description. Just follow the blaze shape and color you have been following and you will have no trouble. The blazes on the old section will have been removed, if metal or plastic markers, or painted black, if painted blazes. We have to note that, unlikely as it sounds, a few persons have faithfully followed painted-out blazes for miles before they woke to the change. Since the old and new sections eventually rejoin, if you are absent-minded yet keen-sighted enough to have this happen to you, you might as well continue to follow the painted-out blazes.

C. WILDERNESS MANNERS

We think that hikers who will be using this book really need no lesson in wilderness manners. To paraphrase W. C. Fields, people who hike can't be all bad! Still, as a refresher, here is our version.

In brief, wilderness manners are simply the Golden Rule applied to the particular circumstances of the countryside. You are sharing the environment with many others—private landowners and users of public land—and you should be sensitive to their rights and needs.

Carry in, carry out—bring out your own litter. You might, on occasion, carry out others' litter, too.

Keep dogs under control, on a leash near livestock or people.

Never smoke while hiking; smoke only when sitting. Be sure your match is out, then bury its head in gravel or dirt. Be sure that what you are smoking is also completely out after you finish it, and bury it in gravel or dirt before you move on.

Do not make fires except in places designated for them. In an emergency, if you must have a fire, build it on rock, gravel or dirt. Forest duff (the normal forest floor made from generations of fallen leaves) is easily ignited and will continue to smolder for days and then burst into flame, so clear the fire area of this material. Keep the fire small, be careful that its sparks do not set a fire elsewhere and thoroughly drench it with water before you leave.

Keep to the paths. Especially avoid cutting across switchbacks on steep hillsides (to prevent erosion); stepping on fragile plants at the higher elevations (which take decades to recover); and walking across farmland and other property (destructive to planting and the goodwill that allows you to be there).

D. WILDERNESS SAFETY

We are ambivalent about safety. On the one hand, we agree with our transatlantic neighbors that Americans are overly concerned about safety. On the other hand, we ourselves are basically cowards and therefore personally cautious. So ignore us as you wish.

Take adequate clothing (see Note E). We never see hikers casually venturing into high country in the summer, clad only in sneakers, shorts and a cotton shirt, without remembering the times high winds and cold rain have swooped down on us out of a hot summer's day.

Don't walk alone. The obvious advantage to this rule is that someone can go for help if you are injured. Less obvious is the psychological boost a companion or two can provide when the going gets tough.

File a hike plan; tell somebody where you are going and when you expect to arrive. No one will ever come looking for you if you get lost or have had an accident if nobody knows you are missing. As a corollary, when you do get safely through, especially if greatly delayed, let that somebody know so that an unnecessary rescue operation isn't undertaken.

E. WHAT TO WEAR AND WHAT TO CARRY

The basics are your boots and socks, raingear and proper warm clothes, the correct map and compass. A first-aid kit, knife, matches, food, whistle and flashlight are emergency basics, most of which we hope you will not have to use. A knapsack is of course necessary, but as long as it is not too big and heavy (you are not going backpacking, only knapsacking), any kind that suits you will be fine. Experts agree that boots should be the best you can afford, a good fit and well broken in before you go. You should wear two pairs of socks, a lightweight wool one next to your skin and a heavier one on the outside. Carry at least one complete change of both kinds.

Besides boots and socks the only articles of clothing on which experts do not have big disagreements are your shirt and light sweater. Any kind or style is OK. But when it comes to what you choose for your warmest garment, how you clothe your legs or what raingear you take, there is a wide variety of preferences. For the first item, down is lightest and warmest, but it loses all its warmth when wet; wool is heaviest and gets still heavier when wet, but continues to keep you warm; the new synthetic fibers are supposed to be both light and warm even when wet, but you get less warmth than for the same weight in down. If your favorite old heavy sweater is a must, remember dirt can cut down on wool's warmth.

For your legs, many swear by jeans or long trousers. We prefer knickers and long socks in cool weather, shorts or a short kilt in hot. The reasons are three: long pants are more restricting when climbing, especially when wet; they get muddier and wetter (especially at the bottom) and take more time and space to dry;

also a spare pair of socks takes less room in your pack than spare hiking trousers.

In raingear, like boots, one tends to get what one pays for. Gore-Tex is expensive but theoretically it lets inside moisture out while keeping rain out, a big asset. However, seams must be sealed adequately; in the cheaper models they are not and sealing is difficult to do for yourself properly. Gore-Tex is probably overrated when put against top-quality lightweight marine foul-weather gear for keeping you dry in a downpour, but it does breathe and works well for us in a light shower. Some people are partial to seamless ponchos which can cover both you and your pack. We have never liked them because they flap so in any wind and get in your way when climbing. Whatever you choose, get it full enough to go over your bulkiest clothing. It should include a jacket and lightweight rain pants made like pajama bottoms, with wide legs to pull over boots and a drawstring waist to adjust to any combination of sweaters. As important as your rain clothes is a good lightweight waterproof knapsack cover. Nothing is more discouraging than finding at the end of a rainy day your nice change of clothes floating in little pools of water at the bottom of your pack.

This then is your basic hiking wardrobe: boots and socks, shirt and pants to fit the season, a light wool sweater, a heavy sweater or down or fiberfilled jacket, raingear, hat, gloves and extra changes of socks. Not much of this will need to go into your pack. A feather-weight sweater or flannel shirt is handy for in-between temperatures or as an extra underlayer when cold. Women particularly may want to include warm tights. For some of the walks in summer the warm hat, gloves and heavy sweater or jacket can be left at home and bathing suit and spare sleeveless shirt added. A light hat with a brim for the hot sun is also useful. The rest of your pack is now free for your emergency basics (some of which can be shared if hiking with others), your personal wants and your civilized clothes. The only change from this packing plan occurs when you are using unheated huts or walking on beaches. (See appropriate sections.)

Now we come to the cinderella trick of, out of your knapsack, turning yourself from trail-soiled hiker into an acceptable guest at those charming country inns. The secret formula is to keep separate, both in your mind and in your knapsack, what you use for hiking and what you use at the inns. Lower your standards about starting out each day with fresh clean clothes. Be prepared each morning to don your hiking togs in whatever state they arrived the night before (except wet). This saves space and weight in your knapsack.

For women, take casual clothes only; dress up with scarves which take up almost no room or weight. Leave your jewelry home. Bring a neutral cardigan which goes with whatever else you have, a nice pair of lightweight wool slacks and/or a lightweight noncrushable skirt, several blouses and turtlenecks and a pair of moccasins or light flat shoes. For summer keep the cardigan, add a bathing suit and substitute cotton or synthetic material for the wool. You'll be neat, clean and stylish always. For men, much of the above applies. You will not need to carry a jacket, your sweaters sufficing. You will need a good pair of slacks, lightweight wool for cool seasons, cotton or synthetic for summer. Moccasins or similar lightweight foot gear save much carrying weight. Shirts are dealer's choice.

F. OTHER THINGS TO CARRY

FIRST AID KIT—If you are an old backpacker, break yourself of thinking in terms of relatively long-time emergency care. You will be checking in each night at civilization, so all you need carry for is trail emergencies. We only take an elastic bandage, moleskin, bandaids, antiseptic, needle, small scissors and aspirin, along with sunburn cream and a good insect repellent.

FOOD—We depend upon the inns to provide us with trail lunches, and we carry a plastic box for those items we do not want crushed. We also carry a pint thermos each so we can share one for lunch and one for a tea break. One water bottle or canteen does for both of us.

BOOKS—If, like our family, you are bookaholics, remember that you do not have to depend on what you carry for reading material. The inns usually have books or magazines available. We each carry a paperback of either exciting trash or philosophy or poetry and trade them around. A hint for source books: if you can bring yourself to destroy a book, cut out of a paperback nature guide only those pages pertaining to the species of the area in which you hike, and make your own little reference book for all the flora and fauna you may want to identify en route. This cuts space and weight tremendously. Think light. If in doubt, leave it out.

INDEX

Note: The 13 walks are set in bold type, while all overnight points are italicized.

Abbe Museum, 12, 15
Acadia Nature Center, 11
Acadia Park Visitor Center, 10
Accommodations (Note A), 181
Adirondak Loj, 107, 112-115, 117
Adirondack Mt Club (ADK), 107, 111
"Agony Grind", 152
Allaben, 120
Alpine, 131, 133, 134
Appalachian Mt Club (AMC), 21, 25, 122
Appalachian Trail (AT), 57, 65, 97, 143, 173
Arden Mt, 152

Balsam Mt, 124-127
Bar Harbor, 9, 11, 12, 15, 18, 19
Barrack Mt, 95, 96, 103, 105
Bascom Lodge, 65, 66, 68-70
Beach Points, 82
Bearfence Mt, 173-175
Bearfort Mt, 148, 150
Beecher Cascade, 31
Beehive, 11, 13, 14
Belleayre Mt, 124-127
Bellvale Mt, 149-151
Berlin Mt, 65, 70, 71
Berlin Pass, 72
Big Indian, 121-127
Big Meadow Lodge, 172, 173, 175-177
Big Slide Mt, 110, 111, 113, 116
Black Rock, 175
Bloodroot Gap, 60
Blueberry Hill, 56, 60-63
Bolton Mt, 41, 45, 46
Bolton Valley Resort, 41, 43-47
Bombay Hook, 132, 135
Booten Gap, 174, 175
Bowl, The, 11, 12, 14
Boott Spur, 38
Brandon Gap, 58-60
Buchanan Mt, 151, 152
Bulls Bridge, 95, 97, 98
Bushnell Falls, 117

Cabin, The, 48, 49, 52
Cadillac Mt, 15
Cahoon Hollow Beach, 82, 85
Camel's Hump Mt, 41, 43, 45, 116
Camp Hoover, 174
Canal Features, 158
Canoe Rentals, 95, 99, 105
Cape Cod Light, 89, 90
Cape Cod National Seashore, 76
Cape Cod Walk, 74
Carmel Camp, 59
Cascade Lakes, 116
Cascade Mt, 110, 113, 116-118
Cathedral Glen, 126, 127
Cathedral Pines, 100, 102
Cat Rock, 150, 151
Catskills, 121, 125
Catskills Park, 121

Catskills Walk, 120
Cedar Run, 178-180
Centre Bridge, 155, 161
Chittenden, 56, 58-60
Coast Guard Beach, 82, 84, 85
Cold Spring Road, 66, 68, 70
Coltsfoot Mt, 100, 101, 103
Cornwall, 101
Cornwall Bridge, 95, 96, 99-101, 103
Crawford House, 31
Crawford Notch, 25, 30, 31
Crum Kill, 136

Dean Ravine, 95, 103, 105
Delaware Canal Walk, 154
Delaware Canal Museum, 156, 158
Delaware-Raritan Canal, 160
Doane Memorial, 84
Dry Gulch, 97, 98
Dudley's Caves, 101
Dutch Hollow, 149
Dutchmans-breeches, 140
Durham boats, 166
Durham Furnace, 166

Eagle Lake (NH), 27
Eagle Lake (ME), 18, 19
Eagles Crag, 16
Eastern Pinnacles, 150
Eastham, 75, 76, 79, 83
East Middlebury, 56
Easton, 155-157, 167-169
Echo Rock, 101
Edmunds Col, 36
Edson Hill Manor, 41, 48-51, 53
Elkton, 171
Escape Routes, 36

Falls Village, 95
Fisher Gap, 176, 177
Featherbed, The, 16
Fitzgerald Falls, 151
Flora Glen, 73
Fox Hollow, 129
Franconia Notch, 21, 23, 25, 26
Franklin Cliffs, 176, 177
Fremont, John C., 137

Galehead Hut, 23, 26-29
Garden, The, 109-111
Garfield Pond, 27, 28
Garfield Ridge, 27, 28
George Washington Bridge, 133
Giant Ledges, 122, 127, 128
Giant Staircase, 96, 98
Gibbs Brook Scenic Area, 31
Golden Pheasant Inn, 155, 157, 161, 163
Gorham Mt, 13
Goshen, 56, 160
Green Mts, 59
Great Dunes, 92
Great Gulf, 34-36

Hiking From Inn to Inn

Greenleaf Hut, 23, 25-27
Green River, 68
Greenwood Lake, 144, 145, 148, 149, 152, 153
Greenwood Lake Village, 143, 144, 149, 150
Greylock Walk, 64
Gull Pond, 87

Hadlock Pond, 17-19
Haley Farm, 70
Haynes Mt, 127
Haverstraw, 131, 139, 140
Hawksbill Gap, 176, 177, 180
Hawksbill Mt, 176
Hazeltop Mt, 173-175
Head of the Meadow, 82, 91
Heart Lake, 108, 109, 111, 113, 114
Hermit Lake, 38, 39
High Gutter Point, 135
High Head, 92, 93
Highland Beach, 82, 90
High Peaks Walk, 106
High Tor, 131, 139, 140, 141
Hook Mt, 139, 141
Hopper, 65, 70, 72
Horrid Cliffs, 59
Housatonic River, 95-97, 99
Housatonic Walk, 94

Johns Brook Lodge, 107-109, 111-113
Jonesville, 41, 43, 44
Jordan Pond, 9, 15-17
Jordan Pond House, 15-17

Keene, 107, 109, 118
Keene Valley, 107-111, 116, 117
Kent, 95-100
Kintnersville, 166
Klondike Notch, 111-113

Lake Dunmore, 60
Lake Mansfield, 47
Lakes of the Cloud Hut, 23, 32-35
Lamont-Doherty Observatory, 136
Lehigh Canal, 158, 167, 169
Lehigh River, 168, 169
Leicester Hollow, 61
Lewis Mt, 171-175
Lime Rock Race Track, 103
Lion Head, 38
Little Porter Mt, 116, 117
Little Tor, 140
Long Clove, 124, 127
Long House Creek, 148
Long Nook Beach, 82, 90
Long Pond, 86
Long Path, 134, 137
Long Trail (LT), 41, 43, 44, 55, 57-60
Lookout Point, 105
Lost Clove, 124, 127
Lower Cape, 76, 87, 91
Lowe's Bald Spot, 37
Luce Hill, 43, 45, 47-49, 52
Luge, 113, 114
Lumberton, 162, 163
Lumberville, 155, 162, 163
Luray, 171, 177, 178

Madison Hut, 24, 37

mail rocket, 145
Mansfield Walk, 40
Maple Grange, 146
Marcy Dam, 118
Mayflower, 76
Michigan Brook, 46
Milam Gap, 175
military road, 119
Mizpah Spring Hut, 23, 30, 31
Mohawk Mt, 95, 100
Mombasha High Point, 151, 152
Mombasha Lake, 151
Monticello Lawn, 35
Morris-Essex Canal, 145
Mountain Road, 48, 50-53
Music Mt Road, 105
Mt Adams, 36
Mt Algo, 98
Mt Carmel, 60
Mt Champlain, 11, 12
Mt Clay, 35
Mt Clinton, 23, 32, 33
Mt Desert Island, 9
Mt Desert Walk, 8
Mt Eisenhower, 32, 33
Mt Fitch, 68
Mt Franklin, 33
Mt Garfield, 27, 28
Mt Greylock, 65-68, 70
Mt Guyot, 28, 29
Mt Jefferson, 35
Mt Lafayette, 26-28
Mt Lincoln, 26
Mt Madison, 34, 36, 37
Mt Mansfield, 41, 42, 52, 11
Mt Marcy, 107, 113, 116-118
Mt Monroe, 24, 33
Mt Moosalamoo, 62, 63
Mt Phelps, 118
Mt Prospect, 66, 67
Mt Van Hoevenberg, 112-115
Mt Washington, 24, 28, 32, 34-36
Mt Williams, 67, 68

Nakedtop Mt, 176, 177
Nauset Light, 85
Nebraska Notch, 45, 47
Newcomb Hollow Beach, 82, 87
New Hope, 155-157, 160
newts, 101, 176
Northeast Harbor, 9, 10,15-19
North Rock, 105
North Truro, 75
Nockamixon Palisades, 165
Nyack, 131-133, 136, 138-140
Nyack Missionary College, 138

Oliverea, 121, 123, 125, 127-129
Otter Cliffs, 11, 12, 14
Otter Point, 14
Otter Creek, 9, 11, 14-17
Overlook Mt, 104

Palisades, 131
Palisades Park, 132
Palisades Walk, 130
Pamet Beach, 82, 88
Pearl Cascade, 31

190

Pemigawasett Wilderness, 21, 23, 28
Peter Buck, 151
Petersburg Pass, 66, 72, 73
Phillips Mill, 155, 161
Piermont, 131-134, 136, 137, 139, 140
Pilgrim Springs, 91
Pilgrim Lake, 80, 89, 92
Pine Hill, 121-127
Pinkham Notch, 21, 25
Pinkham Notch Camp, 24, 37-39
Pollack Knob, 176
Point Pleasant, 155, 162, 163
Porter Mt, 110, 113, 116, 117
Presidential Range, 21
Presidential Range Walk 20, 25
Prospect Rock, 149, 150
Province Lands Visitor Center, 93
Provincetown, 77, 80, 92, 93
Public Transportation (Note A), 181

Race Point Beach, 93
Ramapo, 140, 148, 149, 152
Ranch Camp, 49, 50
Rattlesnake Den, 97, 98
Rapidan River, 171
Riegelsville, 155, 157, 164, 166, 167
Rob George Saddle, 49
Rockland Cemetery, 137
Rockland Lake, 140
Roosevelt State Park, 156

Salt Pond Visitor Center, 77, 83
Sand Beach, 12-14
Sargent Mt, 18
Schaghticoke Mt, 97
Shandaken, 121, 123, 127, 129
Shawangunks, 147
Shenandoah Walk, 170
Sherburne Pass, 56, 57
Sherburne Walk, 54
Short Clove, 139, 140
Sieur de Monts Spring, 11, 12, 14
Silver Lake, 60-62
Skyland Circuit Hike, 179
Skyland Lodge 171, 172, 176, 177
Skyland Road, 177
Skyline Drive, 172-174
Skytop, 49
Slant Rock, 117, 118
Sloan-Stanley Museum, 96
Smithtown, 163
South Meadow, 114
South Meadow Farm Lodge, 107, 109, 115-117
South Pond, 58
South Twin Mt, 29

Southwest Harbor, 10
Spar Kill, 133
Stanley, 171, 178, 179
Star Lake, 24, 37
Stimson Mt, 44
Stowe (village), 41-43, 52, 53
Surprise Lake, 148, 152

Taconic Crest Trail, 65, 70
Taintor Gate, 158, 162, 167
Tallman Mt, 136
Tanners Ridge Fire Rd, 178
Tarn, The, 11, 12, 14
Thayer Ravine, 98
Thompson-Neely House, 159, 160
Three Brothers Mts, 110, 111
Thunder Hole, 11, 14
Tinicum Park, 164
Trailkeeping (Note B), 184
Trailblazing, 184
Truro, 74, 75, 80, 86, 88, 89
Truro Highlands, 77
Tuckerman Ravine, 25, 38, 39
turkeys, 69
Tweed Blvd, 138, 139
Tyler Lake, 95, 96, 100, 102, 103

Upper Black Eddy, 155, 165

Vernon, 147

Walking Purchase, 163
Warwick Turnpike, 143, 150
Washington, 159, 166
Washington Crossing State Park, 159-161, 166
Wawayanda Mt, 146, 147
Wawayanda Walk, 142
Wellfleet, 75, 77, 79, 83, 86, 87
Wetmore Gap, 60
Whiteoak Canyon, 179, 180
Wilderness Safety (Note D), 185
Wild Gardens of Acadia, 11
Williams Outing Club, 65
Williamstown, 65-68, 70-73
Willowbrook Inn, 143, 144, 147, 148, 150
Winooski River, 41, 43

Yardley, 155, 156, 159
Yelping Hill, 104, 105

Zealand Falls Hut, 23, 25, 29-31
Zealand Notch, 23
Zealand Ridge, 28, 29
Zeacliff Pond, 30

ABOUT THE AUTHORS

Kathleen and David MacInnes are ardent walkers, with extensive experience in the United Kingdom, Canada, Switzerland, Norway, Italy and the United States. David was previously engaged in US naval research and development and world mineral research, and Kathleen was a teacher of history; now they are a free-lance writer and artist team. Somehow they have managed to find the time to raise five sons and one daughter and to coauthor WALKING THROUGH SCOTLAND (David and Charles, 1981).